amigurume pets

MAKE CUTE
CROCHET ANIMALS

amiguru**me**

pets

Allison Hoffman

LARK
New York

New York

An Imprint of Sterling Publishing Co., Inc.
1166 Avenue of the Americas
New York, NY 10036

LARK CRAFTS and the distinctive Lark logo are registered trademarks of Sterling Publishing Co., Inc.

ISBN 978-1-4547-0978-7

Library of Congress Cataloging-in-Publication Data

Names: Hoffman, Allison, author.
Title: AmiguruME pets : make cute crochet animals / Allison Hoffman.
Description: New York : Lark, 2017. | Includes index.
Identifiers: LCCN 2016030627 | ISBN 9781454709787 (alk. paper)
Subjects: LCSH: Amigurumi--Patterns. | Soft toy making--Patterns.
Classification: LCC TT829 .H6353 2017 | DDC 745.592--dc23 LC record available at
https://lccn.loc.gov/2016030627

Distributed in Canada by Sterling Publishing Co., Inc.
c/o Canadian Manda Group, 664 Annette Street
Toronto, Ontario, Canada M6S 2C8
Distributed in the United Kingdom by GMC Distribution Services
Castle Place, 166 High Street, Lewes, East Sussex, England BN7 1XU
Distributed in Australia by NewSouth Books
45 Beach Street, Coogee, NSW 2034, Australia

For information about custom editions, special sales, and premium and corporate purchases, please contact
Sterling Special Sales at 800-805-5489 or specialsales@sterlingpublishing.com.

Manufactured in China
2 4 6 8 10 9 7 5 3 1

www.larkcrafts.com
www.sterlingpublishing.com

Photography by Chris Bain
Design by Shannon Nicole Plunkett

contents

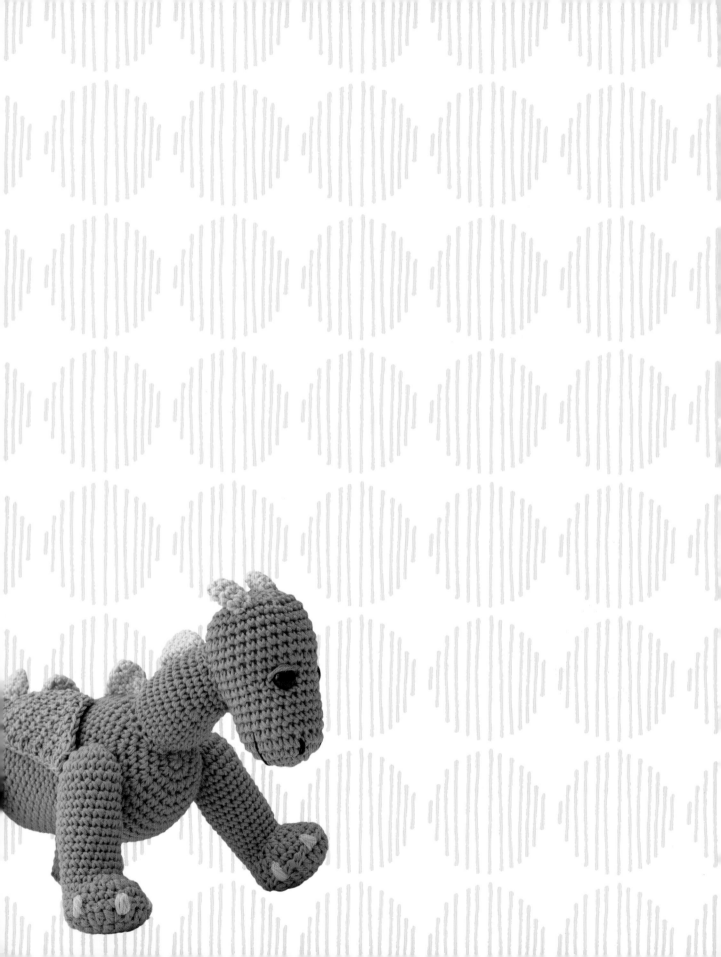

INTRODUCTION

What is it about pets that make our human hearts melt? We love our animals as members of the family. Sure they're sometimes messy, don't listen, and chew up our shoes, and nobody likes emptying a litter box or cleaning a fish tank, but something in us is drawn to their innocent and loyal nature. As a crochet toy designer, I get as many requests for custom pet dolls as I do for custom people dolls. *AmiguruME Pets* finally lets you make a custom crocheted amigurumi of your best animal friend. This book will give you seemingly endless options to create a little replica of your furry (and some not-so-furry) friends.

We'll start with the basics. If you've never crocheted before, you can learn in the How to Crochet section. Starting with materials and tools, I explain step by step exactly what you'll need to make your pet.

The first section of pets is Dogs. By selecting a Head, Ears, Body, Legs, and a Tail, you'll have the ability to create pretty much any breed or mutt you want. Cats are next. Choose from different parts to create your feline friend. Next is Small Pets. These patterns are very short and simple, and include rabbits, hamsters and mice, birds and reptiles. Fantasy Pets, the last section of animals, includes patterns for animals that we all wish we could have. It runs the gamut from a slightly more attainable monkey and pony to the fantastic unicorn and dragon. For a fun element of play, make some things to go with your pet from the Accessories chapter. Here you'll find patterns for collars and tags, beds, tiny toys and bones, and other things your pet needs. This will enable you to personalize the pets even more, especially if you're giving a pet as a gift.

The animals in *AmiguruME Pets* are written to scale with the human dolls in my first book, *AmiguruME: Make Cute Crochet People.* We all know people who are just never without their animal companion, so using *AmiguruME Pets*, your AmiguruME doll doesn't have to be either! If you'd rather, make the pets bigger by increasing hook size and yarn gauge. They'll be bigger and more huggable.

After you've made these sweet animals, there are lots of things you can do with them! Crochet and display your family pets along with crocheted people in your family for a unique family portrait in a shadowbox frame. The tiniest pets can be used as keychains if you attach a short cord and split ring. Make Christmas tree ornaments by attaching a short length of ribbon to the top. My favorite thing to do is to simply arrange them on a shelf. They make unique home decor as they are, and what better way to memorialize a pet than with a miniature version you can love forever?

I hope you enjoy using this book to make your own pet. I love our family dogs, Kona and Bear. The truly unconditional love they show, even when I'm in a bad mood, or if I'm having a bad day, stressed out, or just too busy, is unlike any other relationship. They are still always excited to see me, ready for a good ear scratching, belly rub, or just to cuddle up next to me on the couch. I wrote this book in honor of that special bond between pet and pet lover. I hope it allows you to show your pet love in a new way.

getting started

TOOLS

There are several things as an amigurumi artist that you'll need in your arsenal. Basic tools and some fun yarn are all you'll need to create a full menagerie of pets for everyone you know! That is one of the greatest things about making amigurumi. The small amount of yarn needed and the relatively short amount of time it takes to make them, makes amigurumi a great gift sure to please even the most hard to shop for person on your list!

Crochet Hooks

For the patterns in this book, I chose to use a smaller than average hook. Because the animals you will be making will be pretty small, to get a lot of detail, you need to use a small hook.

My favorite hooks are the ones with ergonomic handles. Because of the small detail work involved in many of the AmiguruME Pets patterns, you'll probably also enjoy using a crochet hook that is comfortable to use on tiny stitches.

If using a small hook presents a problem for you, by all means, feel free to increase the size of your hook. When you increase the size of your hook, the stitches will increase in size, and therefore, your animals will too. Going up in size with your hook necessitates using slightly thicker yarn, or the holes in your stitches will be too large and stuffing will show through. As long as you can get a tight, solid fabric, your hook and yarn combination should be fine.

Below are several examples of what you can expect when you choose to increase hook size and yarn gauge. The dog on the left is made using lightweight yarn and a C hook, as called for in the patterns in the book. The dog on the right is made using worsted-weight yarn and an E hook. The dog in the middle is made using a super bulky weight yarn and an H hook. You could go even smaller or larger, using the same patterns, and come up with even more variety!

Needles

In most of the patterns, you will be instructed to use a yarn needle and an embroidery needle. Stitching animals together with yarn will necessitate using a yarn needle, which has a blunt tip and is used between stitches. An embroidery needle is used for adding details, like mouths, with embroidery floss.

Scissors

A good pair of sharp scissors is absolutely necessary. You'll be snipping yarn and embroidery floss, as well as felt details.

Slicker Brush

A pet brush with lots of tiny metal bristles, called a "slicker brush," is a great tool for brushing yarn surfaces. Any time you want a furry surface, brush each piece gently with a slicker brush before assembling pieces. If you assemble the animal first, it is harder to get in tight spots and it sometimes pulls seams apart. Acrylic or wool blend yarns usually work best with this technique, instead of smoother cotton yarns.

Other Tools

Good quality craft glue will work wonders for tiny bits of felt if you don't want to stitch. A long dowel or even a knitting needle will do the trick for stuffing your animals. Stitch markers are indispensable for keeping track of the spiral rounds used in amigurumi.

MATERIALS

Yarn

I think the most fun thing about needlecrafts is the huge variety of yarn. I personally love going to my local yarn shop or a craft store and browsing the aisles just to see what is new. It's such a tactile experience, and when I see new novelty yarns or a unique color or pattern, I instantly start brainstorming what I can use that yarn to make.

In the Pets patterns, I call for a fine gauge yarn. I usually use worsted weight, but for these smaller projects, to get really fine detail and make small parts, I like a lightweight or sport-weight yarn. Luckily there are lots of options available. There are even bouclé textured and fuzzy yarns that work beautifully for making animal furs. When you are looking for yarn, don't forget to look at the baby yarns. Many of them are finer gauge and come in fuzzy textures that work perfectly in these projects.

Stuffing

Use a polyester fiberfill stuffing for your pets. I like to use the softest I can find, as I find it clumps less easily and is better suited for stuffing small pieces. Use a long dowel, knitting needle, or the eraser end of a pencil to stuff narrow pieces like tails and legs, if necessary.

Safety Eyes and Noses

There are so many options available to you for animal eyes and noses. From basic black eyes to iridescent purple cat eyes, and fuzzy black oval noses to triangular pink cat noses, there are hundreds of ways to personalize your pet. In each pattern I've suggested sizes and shapes, and sometimes colors, but substitutions can be made in any case. Placement of each of these is also suggested, as far as which rounds and how many stitches apart they should be, but this is another way you can switch things up for your own pet.

Sometimes it is difficult to tell where you want to place your eyes and nose until the animal is finished. More than once I've inserted and "locked in" safety eyes and washers, only to discover after stuffing and sewing up an animal, that I wish I'd moved them down slightly, or put them closer together. There is a way around this problem! If in doubt, crochet the entire head, then "try on" the eyes and nose after the entire thing is finished. Dab an extremely tiny amount of super glue over the spot you want to insert the eye and or nose, and immediately insert the post of the safety eye, being very careful not to spread the glue. This will hold the eye or nose into place permanently. I would not recommend doing this if the pet will be given to children, as the glue could release and there could be a choking hazard. But for pets that will be on display, I love this trick.

Felt

Sometimes you aren't able to find the perfect eyes or that "just right" nose for your pet. Use felt instead. Cut into shape and simply stitch on with matching thread or glue on with a good quality craft glue. Felt also works well in a situation in which you want to give a pet to a small child and don't want to use any hard plastic pieces. Felt adds nice details when used behind eyes, as in the Parrot or Sloth, or as teeth, or even inside ears. You can even add a few spots with felt by stitching or gluing on small pieces.

Embroidery Floss

Embroidery is an essential addition to your pets. Stitching with embroidery floss you can add toes, mouths, nostrils, or even stripes and spots. I am never without black floss, but I also keep plenty of other colors on hand too.

Markers

This one may surprise you. "Allison, you want me to draw on my precious crocheted pets?!" There are some situations in which embroidering or sewing on felt patches, or changing yarn colors in the middle of the round is just not practical (I'm looking at you,

Dalmatian!). A basic black or brown marker comes in very handy if you want to really personalize your pet. If there is a tiny black spot right above your pup's right eye, get out your marker and dab it on the crocheted version: instant personalization! Even stripes can be effectively recreated with a few strokes of a marker. Some dogs have black pigmented mouths and a few careful swipes of a black marker can accomplish this look well. Go easy at first, as the ink could spread if you press too hard.

HOW TO CROCHET

Before you can start recreating your pets in crochet, you need to learn a couple of basics. If you already know how to crochet, you can move on to Chapter 1 and get started. If you are new to all this amigurumi business, read on!

There are no fancy stitches to learn in order to make the cutest dog or the scariest dinosaur. Lucky for you, amigurumi is made using really simple stitches and techniques.

Hold Your Hook

There are many ways people hold their crochet hooks. The two basic grips are the pencil grip and the overhand grip. Try out both and see which is most comfortable to you. It is hard to switch to a different grip once you've found your favorite. I use the pencil grip.

Now that you've got a hold on your hook, try out some basic stitches. You've got to figure out how to handle the yarn, which for some people presents a challenge at first. Stay with it—you've got this!

Handling Yarn

When you crochet, your hook goes in your dominant hand (are you a righty or a lefty?), and the yarn goes in the other. Some people like to intricately wrap the yarn around their fingers, providing tension that is necessary for even stitches, and some people just let the yarn fall gently over their hands. Whatever is comfortable to you is the right way to do it.

As you work crochet stitches, keep in mind that every time you move the yarn around the hook, referred to as a "yarn over" or "yo," you will wrap the yarn from the back to the front.

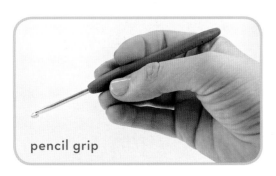

pencil grip

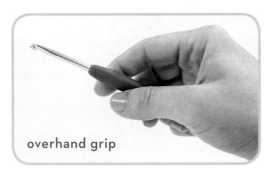

overhand grip

Chain Stitch (ch)

The chain stitch is used as a foundation stitch for crocheting, especially when crocheting something flat in rows. It is also used at the end of rows for turning.

1. To make a chain stitch, begin with a slip knot on your hook. This knot does not count as a stitch but is simply holding the yarn onto your hook for you to do the first stitch (A, B, C).

2. Holding your hook in one hand and with the yarn coming from the ball in the other hand, bring the yarn over the hook (yarn over). It will look like there are two loops of yarn lying over the top of your hook (D).

3. "Catch" the yarn that you just wrapped, and pull it through the first loop on your hook. One loop will remain on your hook, and you've just completed one chain stitch (E)! Repeat steps 2 and 3 for as many chains as the pattern calls for (F).

Each stitch will be a "v" shape. Keep that in mind as you start counting your stitches. The slip knot we started with will not look like a "v" and will not be counted as a stitch. The chain will have a "v" on the front and a little bump on the back. When you start crocheting into a chain, your goal will be to insert your hook between the "v" on top and the bump on the back. This is challenging, even for experienced crocheters, and many people (ahem!) cheat a little and insert the hook into the middle of the "v" for that first row of stitches, or even into the back bar, or bump, of the chain. It leaves a nice lower edge. Try it several ways, and see what is most comfortable for you.

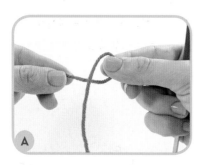

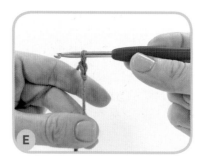

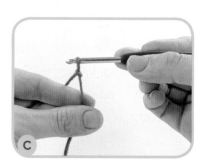

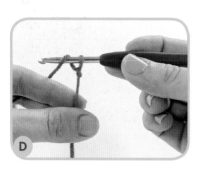

Slip Stitch (sl st)

The slip stitch in crochet is mainly used to move around your work without adding much height to your crocheted piece. It can also be used to join rounds in circular crochet. Because we will be using the Adjustable Ring method for crocheting in the round, which you'll learn next, the slip stitch will be used mainly for fastening off work.

1. Insert the hook into the next stitch. Catch the yarn, without wrapping it around your hook, and pull up a loop.
2. Pull the loop all the way through the loop on your hook. You are left with one loop on your hook, and one slip stitch has been made.

Single Crochet (sc)

Number one stitch to learn? Single crochet. Is the foundation of all amigurumi, as you'll find. It is a small stitch, and very sturdy, so for amigurumi it is perfect to make a dense solid fabric. All the other stitches you'll learn are a variation on the single crochet. The instructions below address crocheting into stitches. Of course when you start, you will crochet into a chain (for rows in flat projects) or a ring (for rounds). Try out a few rows of single crochet just to get a feel for it. You'll be an expert in no time.

1. Insert your hook into the front of the stitch (or chain), under both loops of the stitch (or chain) **(A)**, and pull a loop through to the front. Two loops are on your hook **(B)**.
2. Wrap the working yarn around your hook. There are three loops on your hook **(C)**. Pull the last loop through the first two loops. Only one loop remains on the hook. This is one single crochet stitch **(D)**.

Adjustable Ring Method

Making an adjustable ring only requires a few extra steps and will give your in-the-round projects a smooth start. There are alternative ways to start crocheting in the round, but other methods leave tiny holes. The chain stitch you just learned will be used only once, in the very beginning, but it is a key element.

1. Begin by making a small ring or loop with the yarn, crossing the end of the yarn over the front of the working yarn, leaving a 6-inch (15-cm) tail (A). This ring will be closed in the last step.

2. Hold where both strands of yarn overlap along the ring, keeping the working yarn behind the ring. Moving from front to back, insert your crochet hook into the ring (B), and pull up a loop from the working yarn (C). Make one chain stitch (ch) by yarning over from back to front and pulling through the loop on your hook. There will be one loop on your hook (D, E).

3. Insert your crochet hook back into the ring (F). Pull a loop of working yarn through the center of the ring (G).

4. Now there are two loops on your crochet hook. Yarn over and pull through

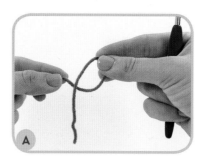

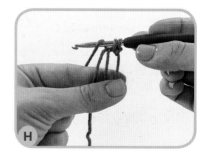

both loops, completing a single crochet stitch (sc) (H, I).

Continue crocheting around both the tail and the ring, repeating steps 3 and 4, until you have the desired number of single crochet stitches (J). When you do, gently pull on the yarn tail to close up the ring. The ring of stitches you have just created will be the base for all of the rest of your stitches and counts as the first round.

Half Double Crochet (hdc)

Half double crochet stitches are exactly what they imply. They are half of a double crochet stitch, which you'll learn next. They are a little taller than a single crochet.

1. Before inserting your hook under the stitch, yarn over (A). Continue on as if you were going to make a single crochet.

Insert your hook under the "v" of the next stitch (B) and pull up a loop. Now you will have three loops on your hook (C).

2. Wrap the working yarn around your hook (D). There are four loops on your hook. Pull the last loop through the first three loops. Only one loop remains on the hook. This completes one half double crochet stitch (E).

Double Crochet (dc)

Double crochet stitches are twice as tall as a single crochet.

1. Wrap the yarn around the hook (yarn over) **(A)**, and insert your hook into the next stitch **(B)**. Pull up a loop. Three loops will be on your hook **(C)**.

2. Yarn over **(D)** and pull the yarn through the first two loops on the hook **(E)**. Two loops will be on the hook.

3. Yarn over again **(F)** and pull the yarn through the last two loops on the hook. There will be one loop on the hook. One double crochet stitch has been made **(G)**.

Triple Crochet (trc)

Triple crochet stitches are three times as tall as a single crochet.

1. Wrap the yarn around the hook twice (yarn over), and insert your hook into the next stitch. Pull up a loop. Four loops will be on your hook.

2. Yarn over and pull the yarn through the first two loops on the hook. Three loops will be on the hook.

3. Yarn over and pull the yarn through the first two loops on the hook. Two loops will be on the hook.

4. Yarn over again and pull the yarn through the last two loops on the hook. There will be one loop on the hook. One triple crochet stitch has been made.

Bobble Stitch

The bobble stitch is used a time or two for thumbs, like in the Monkey, page 131. It creates a small round bump in the round. Several double crochets are used. You will see this in patterns written like this:

bobble [5 dc]

1. Yarn over (A) and insert the hook into the next stitch (B). Pull up a loop (C). Three loops will be on the hook.

2. Yarn over (D) and pull through just two loops. Two loops remain on your hook (E).

3. Repeat steps 1 and 2 into the same stitch (F) until you've made the required number of double crochets as indicated in brackets: [ ]. Each time step 2 is completed, there will be one more loop on your hook. When you've made the required number of double crochets, the number of loops on your hook will be one more than the number of double crochets you made. For example, if the pattern calls for bobble [5 dc], you will have six loops on your hook (G).

A

B

C

D

E

F

4. Yarn over (H) and pull through all the loops on your hook. One loop remains on your hook, and you've made one bobble stitch (I).

5. When you crochet into the next stitch, the bobble stitch you just made will puff out (J). You may need to help the bobble puff out to the right side of the fabric by gently pushing it to the outside.

Increasing

Increasing in crochet is very simple. You will crochet two stitches into one stitch. Increases in rounds are spaced evenly, as written in each pattern. A note about increasing in rounds: by staggering the increases, the finished piece will have a rounder shape. For example, crocheting a few stitches before beginning an increase repeat will make the increase blend in easily, while stacking the increases, or increasing in the same spot in each round, is more noticeable.

Decreasing

To decrease, you have a couple of options.

Single Crochet Two Together (sc2tog)

You may single crochet two stitches together (sc2tog) by inserting your hook into the next stitch (A), pulling up a loop (B), inserting into the next stitch (C) and pulling up another loop (D), and then yarning over (E) and pulling the loop through all the loops on your hook. One loop remains and you have created one sc2tog decrease (F). This is the traditional method used but may leave tiny gaps before and after the stitch. When working in rows, I like to use the sc2tog decrease.

Invisible Decrease (invdec)

Another method of decreasing is the invisible decrease. This creates a less noticeable stitch and is a favorite of amigurumi lovers. Moving your hook from the front to the back of each stitch,

insert your hook into the front loop only of the next two stitches (G), and pull a loop up through both (H). Two loops are

on your hook. Yarn over (I) and pull through both loops. One loop remains on your hook, and you have made one invdec.

Crocheting into Back Loops Only (BLO) or Front Loops Only (FLO)

In most instances, each stitch is crocheted under both loops of the stitch. Sometimes it's necessary to crochet only into one loop of the stitch. This creates a little ridge on the front or back of the work, depending on which loop you crochet into, and makes a stretchier and somewhat thinner fabric. When a pattern calls for crocheting into the back loops only, or BLO, you will insert your hook into the middle of the "v" of the stitch, under only the back of the stitch **(A)**.

If the pattern tells you to crochet into the front loops only, or FLO, you will insert your hook into the front of the stitch, under only the front loop, and out through the middle of the "v" **(B)**.

Changing Color

There will come a time when you're crocheting that you either want to change colors or run out of yarn and need to add yarn from a new ball. It is quite simple to perform a quick change without making a single knot.

the yarn tails on top of the stitches and crocheting over them several times. Clip them with several inches of length left over. After finishing the piece you are working on, you can weave in the ends with a yarn needle.

1. Work the last stitch before the change until the last step of the stitch, just before your last yarn over **(A)**.

2. Instead of finishing the stitch with the old yarn, drop it to the back and pull a loop of the new yarn through the remaining loops on the hook **(B)**. Continue to the next stitch with the new yarn **(C, D)**.

To secure the two ends, continue crocheting, laying

Customize Your Colors

Looking through this book, you're going to see lots of different animals that use more than one color of yarn. The patterns are all written so that whenever and wherever in the course of making your pet, you can change color. You might want to change color somewhere within the body, giving your cat a white belly, for example, or make the tip of your dog's tail a different color than the rest, which is perfect for a Beagle. Your Pony's muzzle may need to be a different color than the rest of her head, or your custom Snake might need stripes. Follow instructions for changing color to customize your pet's coloration however you'd like. No two animals have identical coloring, and the sky's the limit with the number of different colors you can use.

Fastening Off

All done? Time to fasten off.

Simply finish your last stitch, cut the yarn about 6 inches (15 cm) away from the stitch, and hook the strand, pulling it all the way through the loop on your hook.

When working in the round, after completing your final stitch, insert your hook into the next stitch (A), hook the strand (B), and pull it all the way up through the loop on  your hook (C, D). This is a slip stitch (sl st) and makes a smooth edge finish.

Finish by weaving in the yarn tail with a yarn needle. For stuffed toys, the end can be hidden inside the toy. Insert the needle into the toy all the way through to the other side, pulling tightly. Clip the yarn tail close to the surface, and let go, and the yarn tail will retract, hiding itself inside.

Special Amigurumi Techniques

There are several non-crochet techniques you'll need to learn that are unique to making amigurumi.

Stuff It

In the Materials section we discussed the all-important stuffing that goes into your amigurumi pets. Forget what you've always heard about "less is more." The opposite is true. More is more! Because of the nature of the fluffy fiberfill, over time it will compress and any space you've left inside your doll will cause it to lose its shape. Amigurumi should be filled with as much stuffing as you can fit in as long as you are not stretching the fabric so that the stuffing is showing through the holes. If you think you've fit in as much stuffing as you can, try a little more. You may be surprised at how quickly you'll go through a big, 20-ounce (560 g) bag of stuffing!

The smallest pieces you'll be stuffing are your pets' arms and legs. If you wait until the end, you may have a tight squeeze. If you want to avoid this, stuff a little as you go. If you don't have that kind of patience and you want to get it all crocheted at once and worry about stuffing later (like me!), you'll want to stuff those tiny appendages with a knitting needle, a chopstick, or maybe even the end of your crochet hook. Use tiny bits at a time or it will bunch up beyond repair. Then you'll be trying to figure out how to pull those big, wadded-up pieces of stuffing out without ruining your work! Can you tell I am writing from experience?

Construct It

When you've crocheted the pieces of your pet, stuffed them, and you're ready to stick them together, what's next? You need to start construction of what will be your AmiguruME Pet.

Use long straight pins to hold the pieces together; then sew the body parts together using matching yarn and a yarn needle. Many times the stitches will line right up, and you can sew stitch to stitch, creating a seamless join. Most of the time, however, you're going to need to sew as discreetly as possible, up through one piece, out, back down through the other piece, out, and so on. Try not to split the yarn by sewing between stitches instead of through them. When you're finished, you can pull the yarn tightly, knot it close to the surface, let it retract back inside, and then weave the yarn back out through another spot. This will hide the knot inside and redirect the tail from coming out in the same spot.

Crocheting Fur

There are lots of fur yarns available, but unless you are making a huge animal, it is impractical to use these yarns to make small AmiguruME Pets because of their bulky gauge. Instead of using fur yarns, I've found a couple of ways to achieve a furry surface.

The first way to make a fur on your pet is to use either an acrylic or wool blend yarn and a slicker brush, as described in the Tools section (page 1). Brush each individual part before assembly. Rough it up until the stitches are practically hidden or until you are happy with the fuzziness you've achieved. Smooth cotton yarns won't get the furry texture you are looking for.

Another way to get a furry texture, which is especially good for long haired pets, is to hook individual strands of yarn or even embroidery floss into each stitch where you want long hair. This may sound like a tedious prospect, but because these projects are relatively small, the results are well worth the time it may take. A good example of this technique is the Yorkshire Terrier (pictured on page 44) and the Golden Retriever (pictured on page 33). The Yorkshire Terrier's fur is simply hooked into place and left to "flow," while the Golden Retriever has strands hooked and then brushed gently with a slicker brush.

To lock strands of yarn or floss in place, simply insert your crochet hook into the stitch, pull up a loop of new yarn, then pull the ends through loop. Trim as desired. Repeat in the next stitch.

EMBROIDERY HOW-TO

When you're finished crocheting your amigurumi, you'll want to add some embroidery for facial features, markings on the animals' coats, and other details. A few stitches are all you need for some interesting and effective details.

french knot

A French knot is a great stitch for making tiny eyes (like for the Hamster, Mouse, or Fish), spots, or markings. Pull the needle up; wrap thread around the needle two or three times; and insert the needle close to where it came out. Tighten the thread with your other hand, forming a knot, while pulling the thread through to the back.

back stitch

For a thin outline, use a back stitch. The stitches are small and even. Working from right to left, make a short stitch. Pull the needle back up a stitch ahead, and then insert it back down at the beginning of the first stitch. Continue working, connecting stitches backward.

straight stitch

For simple eyelashes or other disconnected stitches, use a straight stitch of any length.

stem stitch

For bolder outline stitches, a stem or an outline stitch is appropriate. Working from left to right, make a small stitch. Keep the thread always on the same side of the needle, and bring the needle up where the last stitch went in, following where you want a line, curved or straight.

dogs

What would we humans do without these furry, four-legged creatures? Dogs aren't called man's best friend for nothing. How many times has your dog gotten mad at you? Held a grudge? Told you your shoes don't match your bag, or questioned why you've been on a Netflix binge all day when you're supposed to be working on a deadline or doing laundry?

These sweet animals deserve our love and affection, and what better way to immortalize them than to make a soft miniature replica in yarn? In the following pages, you'll find patterns for different doggy parts, from heads and ears to tails, so you can make your pedigree bred hound or your one-of-a-kind lovable mutt.

heads

There are lots of things that differentiate dogs from each other, but perhaps nothing shows differences more than head shape. Over the centuries, dogs have been bred for different purposes, and usually one of the most notable things is the shape of the head.

Starting with a Blocky Head, in both small and large versions, you'll find an assortment of head shapes for your dog. Small and Large Pointed Heads and Standard Heads follow. Choose whichever one most closely resembles your dog and the size that is the most accurate. Each pattern features a head and a muzzle, sometimes as one piece, as well as instructions for eye and nose placement. Eye colors are totally up to you, and patterns include recommendations for the eye size as well as nose sizes. I love the look of the ready-made little animal noses available, but you can achieve a sweet handmade look with an embroidered version. You may be surprised at how these little details really bring your canine to life!

Small Blocky Head

This head is just as the name implies: small and square. Know a little Pug or Boston Terrier? This may be the head you choose. If you'd like the muzzle and nose to be extended forward a bit, add a little stuffing around the nose, and pull the muzzle out a little as you stitch. Crochet the head and muzzle in different colors if you'd like, then add the chin piece last for the bottom jaw.

INSTRUCTIONS

Head:

Rnd 1: Starting at top of head, make an adjustable ring, ch 1, work 6 sc into ring. Pull closed—6 sts. Insert a stitch marker into the loop on your hook. Each time you come back around to the stitch marker, move it up to the loop on your hook to begin the next round.

Rnd 2: Work 2 sc into each st around—12 sts.

Rnd 3: *2 sc into next st, sc into next st ; rep from * to end of rnd—18 sts.

Rnd 4: *2 sc into next st, sc into next 2 sts; rep from * to end of rnd—24 sts.

Rnds 5–8: Sc into each st around.

Rnd 9: *Invdec, sc into next 6 sts; rep from * to end of rnd—21 sts.

Rnd 10: Sc into each st around.

Rnd 11: *Invdec, sc into next 5 sts; rep from * to end of rnd—18 sts.

Rnd 12: Sc into each st around.

Rnd 13: *Invdec, sc into next st; rep from * to end of rnd—12 sts.

- Insert safety eyes between Rnds 8 and 9, 5 sts apart. Stuff head firmly and continue.

Rnd 14: Invdec around—6 sts.

- Fasten off with a slip stitch into the next sc, and leave a very long tail. Weave yarn tail through the last round of stitches, and pull tight to close the hole. Weave tail through to back of the bottom of the head and clip.

Muzzle:

Rnd 1: Ch 6. Sc in 2nd ch from hook and next 3 chs, 5 sc in l ch, working into opposite side of beginning ch, sc into next 4 chs, 5 sc into beginning ch—18 sts.

Rnd 2: Sc into each st around.

MATERIALS AND TOOLS

Lightweight yarn in the fur color(s) of your choice (refer to page 159 for a list of recommended yarns) (3)

Black embroidery floss

Crochet hook: 2.75 mm (size C-2 U.S.)

Stitch marker

Yarn needle

Embroidery needle

8-mm safety eyes, color of your choice

7-mm plastic animal nose

Polyester fiberfill stuffing

STITCHES AND TECHNIQUES USED

Adjustable ring, page 8

Chain (ch), page 6

Single crochet (sc), page 7

Invisible decrease (invdec), page 12

Slip stitch (sl st), page 7

(Optional) Changing color, page 14

Rnd 3: Sc into next 6 sts, 2 hdc into next 3 sts, sc into next 6 sts, 2 hdc into next 3 sts—24 sts.

- Fasten off and leave a long tail. You will have a long oval shape. Insert nose into center of muzzle piece. Follow package directions. Flatten oval long ways, and stitch to face in an upside down "U" shape as shown. Weave in ends.

Chin:

Row 1: Ch 4. Sc into 2nd ch from hook and next 2 chs—3 sts.

- Fasten off and leave a long tail for sewing. Stitch chin under the center of the muzzle. Weave in ends.

Finishing:

- With yarn and a yarn needle, stitch one or two straight stitches across the top of the eye for eyelids.

- With black embroidery floss and an embroidery needle, stitch a straight line down from the nose to just underneath the muzzle.

Large Blocky Head

Making a bully breed, like an English Bulldog or Pit Bull Terrier, or maybe a Rottweiler (shown on page 24)? You'll probably choose the Large Blocky Head for your AmiguruME pet! It's similar to the Small Blocky Head but larger in scale. The muzzle, as with the smaller version, can be extended by simply pulling the snout out further and adding a little stuffing around the nose when sewing the muzzle to the head. Each piece can be crocheted in different colors if you'd like, depending on the coloration of your dog.

Skill Level:
INTERMEDIATE

INSTRUCTIONS

Head:

Rnd 1: Starting at top of head, make an adjustable ring, ch 1, work 6 sc into ring. Pull closed—6 sts. Insert a stitch marker into the loop on your hook. Each time you come back around to the stitch marker, move it up to the loop on your hook to begin the next round.

Rnd 2: Work 2 sc into each st around—12 sts.

MATERIALS AND TOOLS

Lightweight yarn in the fur color(s) of your choice (refer to page 159 for a list of recommended yarns) **(3)**

Black embroidery floss

Crochet hook: 2.75 mm (size C-2 U.S.)

(continued on page 24)

Stitch marker

Yarn needle

Embroidery needle

8-mm safety eyes, color of your choice

9-mm plastic animal nose

Polyester fiberfill stuffing

STITCHES AND TECHNIQUES USED

Adjustable ring, page 8

Chain (ch), page 6

Single crochet (sc), page 7

Invisible decrease (invdec), page 12

Slip stitch (sl st), page 7

(Optional) Changing color, page 14

Rnd 3: *2 sc into next st, sc into next st ; rep from * to end of rnd—18 sts.

Rnd 4: *2 sc into next st, sc into next 2 sts; rep from * to end of rnd—24 sts.

Rnd 5: *2 sc into next st, sc into next 3 sts; rep from * to end of rnd—30 sts.

Rnds 6–10: Sc into each st around.

Rnd 11: *Invdec, sc into next 8 sts; rep from * to end of rnd—27 sts.

Rnd 12: Sc into each st around.

Rnd 13: *Invdec, sc into next 7 sts; rep from * to end of rnd—24 sts.

Rnd 14: Sc into each st around.

Insert safety eyes between Rnds 9 and 10, 6 sts apart. Stuff head firmly and continue.

Rnd 15: Invdec around—12 sts.

Rnd 16: Invdec around—6 sts.

- Fasten off with a slip stitch into the next sc, and leave a very long tail. Weave yarn tail through the last round of stitches, and pull tight to close the hole. Weave tail through to back of the bottom of the head and clip.

Muzzle:

Rnd 1: Ch 10. Sc in 2nd ch from hook and next 7 chs, 5 hdc in last ch, working into opposite side of beginning ch, sc into next 8 chs, 5 hdc into beginning ch—26 sts.

Rnd 2: Sc into each st around.

Rnd 3: Sc into next 9 sts, 2 hdc into next 3 sts, sc into next 10 sts, 2 hdc into next 3 sts, sc in next st—32 sts.

- Fasten off and leave a long tail. You'll have a long oval shape. Insert nose into center of muzzle piece. Follow package directions. Flatten long ways and stitch to face in an upside down "U" shape as shown. Weave in ends.

Chin:

Rnd 1: Make an adjustable ring. Ch 1, sc 6 in ring. Pull tail to close ring.

Rnd 2: 2 sc in next st, sc in next 5 sts—7 sts.

Rnds 3–4: Sc in each st.

- Fasten off and leave a long tail. Flatten and sew under muzzle with yarn needle.

Finishing:

- With yarn and a yarn needle, stitch one or two straight stitches across the top of the eye for eyelids.

- With black embroidery floss and an embroidery needle, stitch a straight line down from the nose to just underneath the muzzle.

Small Pointed Head

A little doggy with a long snout, such as a Pomeranian (shown below), will be a perfect match for this selection, the Small Pointed Head. Crocheted all in one piece, the head and muzzle are seamless. A separate chin piece is sewn underneath for the bottom jaw.

Skill Level:
INTERMEDIATE

INSTRUCTIONS

Head:

Rnd 1: Starting at nose end of head, make an adjustable ring, ch 1, work 6 sc into ring. Pull closed—6 sts. Insert a stitch marker into the loop on your hook. Each time you come back around to the stitch marker, move it up to the loop on your hook to begin the next round.

Rnd 2: *2 sc into next st, sc into next st; rep from * to end of rnd—9 sts.

Rnds 3–4: Sc into each st.

Rnd 5: 2 sc into next st, sc into next 8 sts—10 sts.

Rnd 6: *2 sc into next st, sc into next 4 sts; rep from * to end of rnd—12 sts.

Rnd 7: Sc into next 9 sts, 2 sc into next 3 sts—15 sts.

Rnd 8: *2 sc into next st, sc into next 4 sts; rep from * to end of rnd—18 sts.

Rnds 9–11: Sc into each st.

- Insert nose between starting ring and Rnd 2, and safety eyes between Rnds 6 and 7, 4 sts apart. Stuff head firmly and continue.

Rnd 12: *Invdec, sc into next st; rep from * to end of rnd—12 sts.

Rnd 13: Invdec around—6 sts.

- Fasten off with a slip stitch into the next sc, and leave a very long tail. Weave yarn

MATERIALS AND TOOLS

Lightweight yarn in the fur color(s) of your choice (refer to page 159 for a list of recommended yarns) (3)

Black embroidery floss

Crochet hook: 2.75 mm (size C-2 U.S.)

Stitch marker

Yarn needle

Embroidery needle

6-mm safety eyes, color of your choice

7-mm plastic animal nose

Polyester fiberfill stuffing

STITCHES AND TECHNIQUES USED

Adjustable ring, page 8

Chain (ch), page 6

Single crochet (sc), page 7

Invisible decrease (invdec), page 12

Slip stitch (sl st), page 7

(Optional) Changing color, page 14

tail through the last round of stitches, and pull tight to close the hole. Weave tail through to back of the bottom of the head and clip.

Chin:

Row 1: Ch 4. Hdc into 3rd ch from hook and next ch.

- Fasten off and leave a long tail. Sew under head with yarn needle.

Finishing:

- With yarn and a yarn needle, stitch one or two straight stitches across the top of each eye for eyelids.

- With black embroidery floss and an embroidery needle, stitch a straight line down from the nose to just inside the mouth.

Large Pointed Head

Any dog with a larger head and the same pointy snout, such as a Greyhound or a German Shepherd (shown on page 27), will be a good match for this version. The head and muzzle are seamless, crocheted all in one piece. A chin is crocheted last and sewn on.

Skill Level:
INTERMEDIATE

INSTRUCTIONS

Head:

Rnd 1: Starting at nose end of head, make an adjustable ring, ch 1, work 6 sc into ring. Pull closed—6 sts. Insert a stitch marker into the loop on your hook. Each time you come back around to the stitch marker, move it up to the loop on your hook to begin the next round.

Rnd 2: 2 sc into next st, sc into each st—7 sts.

Rnd 3: 2 sc into next st, sc into each st—8 sts.

Rnd 4: 2 sc into next st, sc into each st—9 sts.

Rnd 5: 2 sc into next st, sc into each st—10 sts.

Rnd 6: 2 sc into next st, sc into each st—11 sts.

Rnd 7: 2 sc into next st, sc into each st—12 sts.

Rnd 8: Sc into next 6 sts, 2 sc

MATERIALS AND TOOLS

Lightweight yarn in the fur color(s) of your choice (refer to page 159 for a list of recommended yarns) **(3)**

Black embroidery floss

Crochet hook: 2.75 mm (size C-2 U.S.)

Stitch marker

Yarn needle

Embroidery needle

8-mm safety eyes, color of your choice

9-mm plastic animal nose

Polyester fiberfill stuffing

Adjustable ring, page 8

Chain (ch), page 6

Single crochet (sc), page 7

Invisible decrease (invdec),
page 12

Slip stitch (sl st), page 7

(Optional) Changing color,
page 14

into next 3 sts, sc into next 3
sts—15 sts.

Rnd 9: *2 sc into next st, sc
into next 4 sts; rep from * to
end of rnd—18 sts.

Rnd 10: *2 sc into next st, sc
into next 2 sts; rep from * to
end of rnd—24 sts.

Rnds 11–14: Sc into each st.

- Insert nose between
starting ring and Rnd 2, and
safety eyes between Rnds 8
and 9, 4 sts apart. Stuff head
firmly and continue.

Rnd 15: *Invdec, sc into next
2 sts; rep from * to end of
rnd—18 sts.

Rnd 16: *Invdec, sc into
next st; rep from * to end of
rnd—12 sts.

Rnd 17: Invdec around—6 sts.

- Fasten off with a slip stitch
into the next sc, and leave

a very long tail. Weave yarn
tail through the last round
of stitches, and pull tight
to close the hole. Weave
tail through to back of the
bottom of the head and clip.

Chin:

Row 1: Ch 5. Hdc into 3rd
ch from hook and next 2 ch.

- Fasten off and leave a long
tail. Sew under head with
yarn needle.

Finishing:

- With yarn and a yarn
needle, stitch one or two
straight stitches across the
top of each eye for eyelids.

- With black embroidery
floss and an embroidery
needle, stitch a straight line
down from the nose to just
inside the mouth.

Small Standard Head

For a small dog with a standard head, not too pointed and not too blocky, you'll want to use the Small Standard Head pattern. This head is made with a separate sewn-on muzzle and will be perfect for breeds ranging from a feisty Yorkie to a loyal Beagle. Each piece can either be crocheted in different colors or all in the same color.

Skill Level:
INTERMEDIATE

INSTRUCTIONS

Head:

Rnd 1: Starting at top of head, make an adjustable ring, ch 1, work 6 sc into ring. Pull closed—6 sts. Insert a stitch marker into the loop on your hook. Each time you come back around to the stitch marker, move it up to the loop on your hook to begin the next round.

Rnd 2: Work 2 sc into each st around—12 sts.

Rnd 3: *2 sc into next st, sc into next st; rep from * to end of rnd—18 sts.

Rnd 4: *2 sc into next st, sc into next 2 sts; rep from * to end of rnd—24 sts.

Rnds 5–6: Sc into each st around.

Rnd 7: *Invdec, sc into next 2 sts; rep from * to end of rnd—18 sts.

Rnds 8–9: Sc into each st around.

- Insert safety eyes between Rnds 8 and 9, 5 sts apart. Stuff head firmly and continue.

Rnd 10: *Invdec, sc into next st; rep from * to end of rnd—12 sts.

Rnd 11: Invdec around—6 sts.

- Fasten off with a slip stitch into the next sc, and leave a very long tail. Weave yarn tail through the last round of stitches, and pull tight to close the hole. Weave tail through to back of the bottom of the head and clip.

Muzzle:

Rnd 1: Make an adjustable ring and ch 1. Sc 6 into ring. Pull tail to close hole.

Rnd 2: *2 sc into next st, sc into next st; rep from * to end of rnd—9 sts.

Rnd 3: *2 sc into next st, sc into next 2 sts; rep from * to end of rnd—12 sts.

MATERIALS AND TOOLS

Lightweight yarn in the fur color(s) of your choice (refer to page 159 for a list of recommended yarns) (3)

Black embroidery floss

Crochet hook: 2.75 mm (size C-2 U.S.)

Stitch marker

Yarn needle

Embroidery needle

6-mm safety eyes, color of your choice

7-mm plastic animal nose

Polyester fiberfill stuffing

STITCHES AND TECHNIQUES USED

Adjustable ring, page 8

Chain (ch), page 6

Single crochet (sc), page 7

Invisible decrease (invdec), page 12

Slip stitch (sl st), page 7

(Optional) Changing color, page 14

Rnds 4–5: Sc into each st.

- Fasten off and leave a long tail. Insert nose into Muzzle between Rnds 1 and 2. Stuff muzzle and sew to head with yarn needle.

Chin:

Rnd 1: Make an adjustable ring and ch 1. Sc 6 into ring. Pull tail to close hole.

Rnds 2–3: Sc into each st.

- Fasten off and leave a long tail. Flatten and sew to head under muzzle.

Finishing:

- With yarn and a yarn needle, stitch one or two straight stitches across the top of each eye for eyelids.

- With black embroidery floss and an embroidery needle, stitch a straight line down from the nose to just inside the mouth.

Large Standard Head

If you're not sure which pattern suits your dog, chances are the Large Standard Head will work. For a Labrador Retriever, Dalmatian, Husky, and anything in between, this head, with a separate sewn on muzzle, will work. Each piece can either be crocheted in different colors or all in the same color. A lower jaw, or chin, is sewn on last. For the Dalmatian (shown on page 30), tiny spots were drawn on with a permanent marker, but you can embroider spots if you'd like!

Skill Level:
INTERMEDIATE

INSTRUCTIONS

Head:

Rnd 1: Starting at top of head, make an adjustable ring, ch 1, work 6 sc into ring. Pull closed—6 sts. Insert a stitch marker into the loop on your hook. Each time you come back around to the stitch marker, move it up to the loop on your hook to begin the next round.

Rnd 2: Work 2 sc into each st around—12 sts.

Rnd 3: *2 sc into next st, sc into next st; rep from * to end of rnd—18 sts.

Rnd 4: *2 sc into next st, sc into next 2 sts; rep from * to end of rnd—24 sts.

MATERIALS AND TOOLS

Lightweight yarn in the fur color(s) of your choice (refer to page 159 for a list of recommended yarns) (3)

Black embroidery floss

Crochet hook: 2.75 mm (size C-2 U.S.)

Stitch marker

Yarn needle

(continued on page 30)

Embroidery needle

8-mm safety eyes, color of your choice

9-mm plastic animal nose

Polyester fiberfill stuffing

(Optional) Black permanent marker

Adjustable ring, page 8

Chain (ch), page 6

Single crochet (sc), page 7

Invisible decrease (invdec), page 12

Slip stitch (sl st), page 7

(Optional) Changing color, page 14

Rnds 5–9: Sc into each st around.

Rnd 10: *Invdec, sc into next 2 sts; rep from * to end of rnd—18 sts.

- Insert safety eyes between Rnds 9 and 10, 6 sts apart. Stuff head firmly and continue.

Rnd 11: *Invdec, sc in next st; rep from * around— 12 sts.

Rnd 12: Invdec around—6 sts.

- Fasten off with a slip stitch into the next sc, and leave a very long tail. Weave yarn tail through the last round of stitches, and pull tight to close the hole. Weave tail through to back of the bottom of the head and clip.

Muzzle:

Rnd 1: Make an adjustable ring and ch 1. Sc 9 into ring. Pull tail to close hole.

Rnd 2: *2 sc into next st, sc into next 2 sts; rep from * to end of rnd—12 sts.

Rnd 3: *2 sc into next st, sc into next 3 sts; rep from * to end of rnd—15 sts.

Rnds 4–5: Sc into each st.

Rnd 6: *2 sc into next st, sc into next 4 sts; rep from * to end of rnd—18 sts.

Rnd 7: *2 sc into next st, sc into next 5 sts; rep from * to end of rnd—21 sts.

- Fasten off and leave a long tail. Insert nose into muzzle between Rnds 1 and 2. Stuff muzzle and sew to head with yarn needle.

Chin:

Rnd 1: Make an adjustable ring and ch 1. Sc 9 into ring. Pull tail to close hole.

Rnds 2–4: Sc into each st.

- Fasten off and leave a long tail. Flatten and sew to head under muzzle.

Finishing:

- With yarn and a yarn needle, stitch one or two straight stitches across the top of each eye for eyelids.

- With black embroidery floss and an embroidery needle, stitch a straight line down from the nose to just inside the mouth.

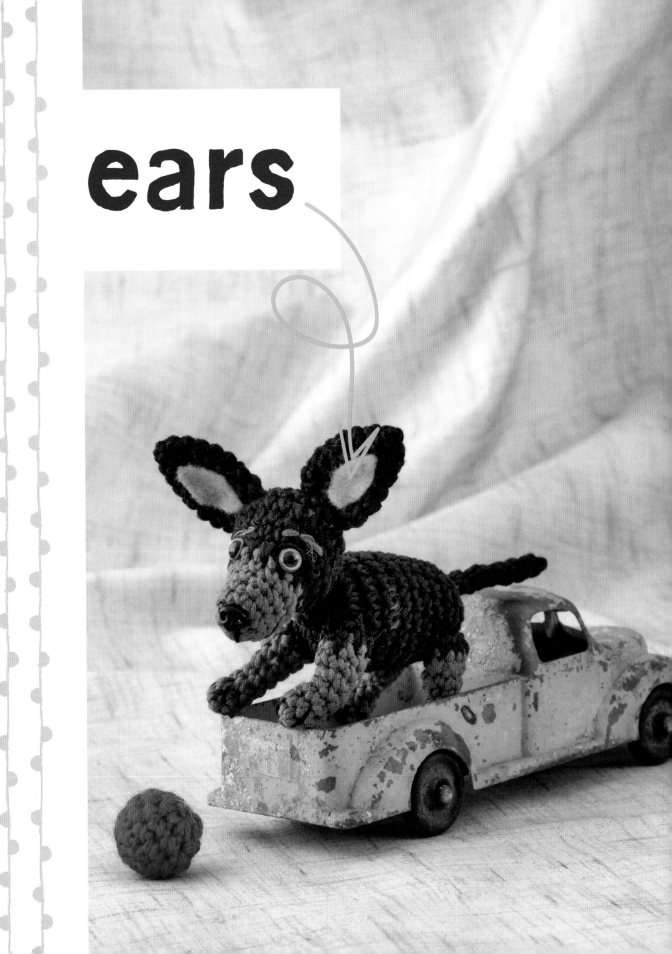

ears

Now that your dog's head has been crocheted, how about a cute pair of ears? Are they long and floppy or short and pointed? Maybe one ear folds down and another sticks up.

The patterns over the next several pages will show you how to make different kinds of classic dog ear shapes. Choose from a Drop Ear, Floppy Ear, Rose Ear, and large or small Pointed Ear.

If you'd like, you can add a little color into the ear with pink blush or black eyeshadow. Rub your pinky into blush or eyeshadow, then in the center of the ear.

Drop Ear

A Drop Ear is a classic folded ear found on Golden Retrievers (shown below), Saint Bernards, Dalmatians, and many other types of dogs. The pattern will create a natural fold at the base of the ear, and the ear length can be extended by repeating the final round if desired.

Skill Level:
INTERMEDIATE

INSTRUCTIONS

Rnd 1: Starting at the tip of the ear, make an adjustable ring, ch 1, and work 4 sc into ring. Pull closed—4 sts. Insert a stitch marker into the loop on your hook. Each time you come back around to the stitch marker, move it up to the loop on your hook to begin the next round.

Rnd 2: Work 2 sc into each st around—8 sts.

Rnd 3: Sc into each st around.

Rnd 4: 2 sc into next st, sc into each st around—9 sts.

Rnd 5: 2 sc into next st, sc into each st around—10 sts.

Rnd 6: *2 sc into next st, sc into next 4 sts; rep from * to end of rnd—12 sts.

Rnd 7: *2 sc into next st, sc into next 5 sts; rep from * to end of rnd—14 sts.

Rnds 8–9: Sc into each st.

Rnd 10: *Invdec, sc in next 5 sts; rep from * to end of rnd—12 sts.

Rnd 11: *Invdec, sc in next 4 sts; rep from * to end of rnd—10 sts.

Note: For a longer ear, repeat Rnd 11 as many times as desired.

- Fasten off with a slip stitch into the next sc, and leave a long tail. Stitch ear to side of head with yarn needle and yarn tail. Repeat for second ear.

MATERIALS AND TOOLS

Lightweight yarn in the fur color(s) of your choice (refer to page 159 for a list of recommended yarns) (3)

Crochet hook: 2.75 mm (size C-2 U.S.)

Stitch marker

Yarn needle

STITCHES AND TECHNIQUES USED

Adjustable ring, page 8

Chain (ch), page 6

Single crochet (sc), page 7

Invisible decrease (invdec), page 12

Slip stitch (sl st), page 7

(Optional) Changing color, page 14

Floppy Ear

Does your dog have ears that hang low? Floppy-eared dogs like Basset Hounds, Dachshunds, and Poodles (shown below) will look great with this ear type. If they're really long, get to the last round and repeat for as long as you'd like.

Skill Level:
INTERMEDIATE

INSTRUCTIONS

Rnd 1: Starting at the tip of the ear, make an adjustable ring, ch 1, and work 6 sc into ring. Pull closed—6 sts. Insert a stitch marker into the loop on your hook. Each time you come back around to the stitch marker, move it up to the loop on your hook to begin the next round.

Rnd 2: *2 sc into next st, sc in next st; rep from * to end of rnd—9 sts.

Rnd 3: *2 sc into next st, sc into next 2 sts; rep from * to end of rnd—12 sts.

Rnd 4: Sc into each st around.

Rnd 5: *Invdec, sc into next 4 sts; rep from * to end of rnd—10 sts.

Rnd 6: Invdec, sc into next 8 sts—9 sts.

Rnd 7: Invdec, sc into next 7 sts—8 sts.

Rnd 8: Invdec, sc into next 6 sts—7 sts.

Rnd 9: Sc in each st around.

Note: For a longer ear, repeat Rnd 9 as many times as desired.

- Fasten off with a slip stitch into the next sc, and leave a long tail. Stitch ear to side of head with yarn needle and yarn tail. Repeat for second ear.

MATERIALS AND TOOLS

Lightweight yarn in the fur color(s) of your choice (refer to page 159 for a list of recommended yarns) (3)

Crochet hook: 2.75 mm (size C-2 U.S.)

Stitch marker

Yarn needle

STITCHES AND TECHNIQUES USED

Adjustable ring, page 8

Chain (ch), page 6

Single crochet (sc), page 7

Invisible decrease (invdec), page 12

Slip stitch (sl st), page 7

(Optional) Changing color, page 14

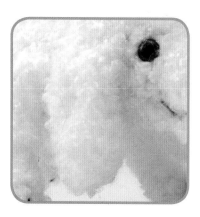

Small Rose Ear

A Rose Ear folds backward instead of forward and gets its name from the shape of the ear at the base, which sometimes resembles a rose. As you crochet it, it will take shape and should be sewn into place with the tip pointed toward the back of the head, which can be tacked into place if desired. This smaller version can be seen on Pugs (shown below), Whippets, and Greyhounds.

Skill Level:
INTERMEDIATE

INSTRUCTIONS

Rnd 1: Starting at the tip of the ear, make an adjustable ring, ch 1, and work 8 sc into ring. Pull closed—8 sts. Insert a stitch marker into the loop on your hook. Each time you come back around to the stitch marker, move it up to the loop on your hook to begin the next round.

Rnds 2–3: Sc into each st around.

Rnd 4: Working into FLO, sc into next 4 sts, working into both loops of each st, sc in next 2 sts, work 2 sc in next st, sc in next st—9 sts.

Rnd 5: Sc into each st around.

Note: For a longer ear, repeat Rnd 5 as many times as desired.

- Fasten off with a slip stitch into the next sc, and leave a long tail. Stitch ear to side of head with yarn needle and yarn tail. Repeat for second ear.

MATERIALS AND TOOLS

Lightweight yarn in the fur color(s) of your choice (refer to page 159 for a list of recommended yarns) **(3)**

Crochet hook: 2.75 mm (size C-2 U.S.)

Stitch marker

Yarn needle

STITCHES AND TECHNIQUES USED

Adjustable ring, page 8

Chain (ch), page 6

Single crochet (sc), page 7

Front loops only (FLO), page 13

Slip stitch (sl st), page 7

(Optional) Changing color, page 14

Large Rose Ear

The Large Rose Ear is the pattern you'll need if you're making a larger bully breed, like a Bulldog (shown below), with ears that fold backward. If desired, tack the tips of the ears so that they'll stay positioned pointing back.

INSTRUCTIONS

Rnd 1: Starting at the tip of the ear, make an adjustable ring, ch 1, and work 8 sc into ring. Pull closed—8 sts. Insert a stitch marker into the loop on your hook. Each time you come back around to the stitch marker, move it up to the loop on your hook to begin the next round.

Rnds 2–5: Sc into each st around.

Rnd 6: Working into FLO, sc into next 4 sts, working into both loops of each st, sc in next 2 sts, work 2 sc in next st, sc in next st—9 sts.

Rnd 7: Sc into each st around.

Note: For a longer ear, repeat Rnd 7 as many times as desired.

- Fasten off with a slip stitch into the next sc, and leave a long tail. Stitch ear to side of head with yarn needle and yarn tail. Repeat for second ear.

MATERIALS AND TOOLS

Lightweight yarn in the fur color(s) of your choice (refer to page 159 for a list of recommended yarns) (3)

Crochet hook: 2.75 mm (size C-2 U.S.)

Stitch marker

Yarn needle

STITCHES AND TECHNIQUES USED

Adjustable ring, page 8

Chain (ch), page 6

Single crochet (sc), page 7

Front loops only (FLO), page 13

Slip stitch (sl st), page 7

(Optional) Changing color, page 14

Small Pointed Ear

A pointed ear, or "prick" ear, is said to be directly inherited from the dog's ancestor, the wolf. From this pattern you can make an ear that stands upright, pointed. If you fold the top of the ear all the way down, it will make a "button ear," commonly found in Jack Russell Terriers and Fox Terriers. Folding half the way down will make a "cocked," or "semi-prick," ear like those found in Collies and some Pit Bulls. Use this smaller ear pattern for Chihuahuas, Westies, Schnauzers (shown below), and any small pointed-ear dog.

INSTRUCTIONS

Rnd 1: Starting at the tip of the ear, make an adjustable ring, ch 1, and work 4 sc into ring. Pull closed—4 sts. Insert a stitch marker into the loop on your hook. Each time you come back around to the stitch marker, move it up to the loop on your hook to begin the next round.

Rnd 2: *2 sc into next st, sc into next st; rep from * to end of rnd—6 sts.

Rnd 3: *2 sc into next st, sc into next 2 sts; rep from * to end of rnd—8 sts.

Rnd 4: 2 sc into next st, sc into next 7 sts—9 sts.

Rnd 5: 2 sc into next st, sc into next 8 sts—10 sts.

Note: For a little longer ear, repeat Rnd 5 as many times as desired.

- Fasten off with a slip stitch into the next sc, and leave a long tail. Pinch base of ear slightly as you stitch ear to side of head with yarn needle and yarn tail. For a button or semi-prick ear, fold down tip and tack into place. Repeat for second ear.

MATERIALS AND TOOLS

Lightweight yarn in the fur color(s) of your choice (refer to page 159 for a list of recommended yarns) (3)

Crochet hook: 2.75 mm (size C-2 U.S.)

Stitch marker

Yarn needle

STITCHES AND TECHNIQUES USED

Adjustable ring, page 8

Chain (ch), page 6

Single crochet (sc), page 7

Slip stitch (sl st), page 7

(Optional) Changing color, page 14

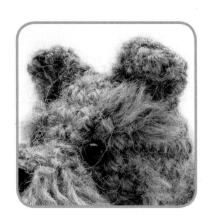

Large Pointed Ear

Use this Large Pointed Ear pattern for Corgis (shown below), German Shepherds, French Bulldogs, or any dog with larger pointed ears. As with the Small Pointed Ear, the tip can be folded down for a button ear or a semi-pricked ear.

INSTRUCTIONS

Rnd 1: Starting at the tip of the ear, make an adjustable ring, ch 1, and work 4 sc into ring. Pull closed—4 sts. Insert a stitch marker into the loop on your hook. Each time you come back around to the stitch marker, move it up to the loop on your hook to begin the next round.

Rnd 2: *2 sc into next st, sc into next st; rep from * to end of rnd—6 sts.

Rnd 3: *2 sc into next st, sc into next 2 sts; rep from * to end of rnd—8 sts.

Rnd 4: *2 sc into next st, sc into next 3 sts; rep from * to end of rnd—10 sts.

Rnd 5: *2 sc into next st, sc into next 4 sts; rep from * to end of rnd—12 sts.

Rnd 6: Sc into each st.

Note: For a little longer ear, repeat Rnd 6 as many times as desired.

- Fasten off with a slip stitch into the next sc, and leave a long tail. Flatten ear and pinch base of ear slightly as you stitch ear to side of head with yarn needle and yarn tail. For a button or semi-prick ear, fold down tip and tack into place. Repeat for second ear.

MATERIALS AND TOOLS

Lightweight yarn in the fur color(s) of your choice (refer to page 159 for a list of recommended yarns) **(3)**

Crochet hook: 2.75 mm (size C-2 U.S.)

Stitch marker

Yarn needle

STITCHES AND TECHNIQUES USED

Adjustable ring, page 8

Chain (ch), page 6

Single crochet (sc), page 7

Slip stitch (sl st), page 7

(Optional) Changing color, page 14

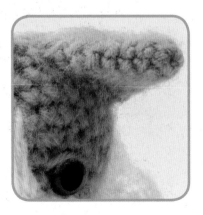

body
shapes

After the head and ears are complete, unless you're going to make a keychain or pendant from that cute mug (not a bad idea!), you'll choose which body type to make for your dog. We'll start with a Stocky Body build, in both small and regular size, as well as Standard Body in small and regular size, and finish up with an Extended Body shape, also in small and regular.

While you're making the body, feel free to incorporate color changes to mimic your dog's specific markings. As simple as an in-round color change, as discussed on page 14, this can be used for adding spots or stripes, or just an all over pattern.

Also as discussed earlier (page 3), different yarns and techniques can be used to achieve the many variations of doggy coat types. A smooth coat will be easy with just a regular smooth yarn. A furry or fuzzy coat can be achieved with either a light bouclé or a simple brushing of a smoother yarn. And a very shaggy coat can be made by hand-hooking strands of yarn all over, as discussed on page 17. These techniques are especially effective on the body portion of your dog.

Small Stocky Body

A Small Stocky Body shape is going to be a little thicker, a little shorter, and perfect for pups like Pugs, Westies (shown below), or French Bulldogs. Since this creates a smaller, stocky dog, there is no separate neck to sew on and the head is attached directly to the body.

Skill Level:
INTERMEDIATE

INSTRUCTIONS

Rnd 1: Starting at front end of body, make an adjustable ring, ch 1, work 6 sc into ring. Pull closed—6 sts. Insert a stitch marker into the loop on your hook. Each time you come back around to the stitch marker, move it up to the loop on your hook to begin the next round.

Rnd 2: 2 sc into each st around—12 sts.

Rnd 3: 2 sc into each st around—24 sts.

Rnds 4–8: Sc into each st.

Rnd 9: *Invdec, sc into next 6 sts; rep from * to end of rnd—21 sts.

Rnd 10: Sc into each st around.

Rnd 11: *Invdec, sc into next 5 sts; rep from * to end of rnd—18 sts.

Rnd 12: Sc into each st around.

Rnd 13: *Invdec, sc into next st; rep from * to end of rnd—12 sts.

- Insert a stitch marker to hold your place. Stuff Body firmly.

Rnd 14: Invdec around—6 sts.

- Fasten off with a slip stitch into the next sc, and leave a long tail. Weave yarn tail through the last round of stitches, and pull tight to close the hole. Sew body to head. Weave in ends.

MATERIALS AND TOOLS

Lightweight yarn in the fur color(s) of your choice (refer to page 159 for a list of recommended yarns) (3)

Crochet hook: 2.75 mm (size C-2 U.S.)

Stitch marker

Yarn needle

Polyester fiberfill stuffing

STITCHES AND TECHNIQUES USED

Adjustable ring, page 8

Chain (ch), page 6

Single crochet (sc), page 7

Invisible decrease (invdec), page 12

Slip stitch (sl st), page 7

(Optional) Changing color, page 14

Regular Stocky Body

This body shape will work well for a dog that is wide and/or muscular. The head is attached directly to the body. Try this pattern for a Saint Bernard (shown on page 43), Bulldog, Rottweiler, Pit Bull, or any muscular dog you know.

INSTRUCTIONS

Rnd 1: Starting at front end of body, make an adjustable ring, ch 1, work 6 sc into ring. Pull closed—6 sts. Insert a stitch marker into the loop on your hook. Each time you come back around to the stitch marker, move it up to the loop on your hook to begin the next round.

Rnd 2: 2 sc into each st around—12 sts.

Rnd 3: *2 sc into next st, sc into next st; rep from * to end of rnd—18 sts.

Rnd 4: *2 sc into next st, sc into next 2 sts; rep from * to end of rnd—24 sts.

Rnd 5: *2 sc into next st, sc into next 3 sts; rep from * to end of rnd—30 sts.

Rnd 6: *2 sc into next st, sc into next 4 sts; rep from * to end of rnd—36 sts.

Rnd 7: *2 sc into next st, sc into next 11 sts; rep from * to end of rnd—39 sts.

Rnds 8–9: Sc into each st.

Rnd 10: *Invdec, sc into next 11 sts; rep from * to end of rnd—36 sts.

Rnd 11: *Invdec, sc into next 10 sts; rep from * to end of rnd—33 sts.

Rnds 12–14: Sc into each st around.

Rnd 15: *Invdec, sc into next 9 sts; rep from * to end of rnd—30 sts.

Rnds 16–17: Sc into each st around.

Rnd 18: *Invdec, sc into next 8 sts; rep from * to end of rnd—27 sts.

Rnds 19–20: Sc into each st around.

Rnd 21: *2 sc into next st, sc into next 8 sts; rep from * to end of rnd—30 sts.

Rnd 22: Sc into each st around.

Rnd 23: *Invdec, sc into next 3 sts; rep from * to end of rnd—24 sts.

MATERIALS AND TOOLS

Lightweight yarn in the fur color(s) of your choice (refer to page 159 for a list of recommended yarns) (3)

Crochet hook: 2.75 mm (size C-2 U.S.)

Stitch marker

Yarn needle

Polyester fiberfill stuffing

STITCHES AND TECHNIQUES USED

Adjustable ring, page 8

Chain (ch), page 6

Single crochet (sc), page 7

Invisible decrease (invdec), page 12

Slip stitch (sl st), page 7

(Optional) Changing color, page 14

Rnd 24: *Invdec, sc into next 2 sts; rep from * to end of rnd—18 sts.

- Insert a stitch marker to hold your place. Stuff body firmly.

Rnd 25: *Invdec, sc into next st; rep from * to end of rnd—12 sts.

Rnd 26: Invdec around—6 sts.

- Fasten off with a slip stitch into the next sc, and leave a long tail. Weave yarn tail through the last round of stitches, and pull tight to close the hole. Sew body to head. Weave in ends.

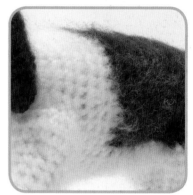

Small Standard Body

For a dog that's of medium weight and build, but short of stature, use the Small Standard Body pattern. If you're making any small medium build dog, from a Yorkie (shown on page 44) to a Beagle, this pattern will work great.

Skill Level:
INTERMEDIATE

INSTRUCTIONS

Rnd 1: Starting at front end of body, make an adjustable ring, ch 1, work 6 sc into ring. Pull closed—6 sts. Insert a stitch marker into the loop on your hook. Each time you come back around to the stitch marker, move it up to the loop on your hook to begin the next round.

Rnd 2: 2 sc into each st around—12 sts.

Rnd 3: *2 sc into next st, sc into next st; rep from * to end of rnd—18 sts.

Rnds 4–7: Sc into each st.

Rnd 8: *Invdec, sc into next 16 sts—17 sts.

MATERIALS AND TOOLS

Lightweight yarn in the fur color(s) of your choice (refer to page 159 for a list of recommended yarns)

Crochet hook: 2.75 mm (size C-2 U.S.)

Stitch marker

Yarn needle

Polyester fiberfill stuffing

(continued on page 44)

Adjustable ring, page 8

Chain (ch), page 6

Single crochet (sc), page 7

Invisible decrease (invdec),
page 12

Slip stitch (sl st), page 7

(Optional) Changing color,
page 14

Rnd 9: *Invdec, sc into next
15 sts—16 sts.

Rnd 10: *Invdec, sc into next
14 sts—15 sts.

Rnd 11: *2 sc into next st, sc
into next 4 sts; rep from * to
end of rnd—18 sts.

Rnd 12: *Invdec, sc into
next st; rep from * to end of
rnd—12 sts.

- Insert a stitch marker to hold
your place. Stuff body firmly.

Rnd 13: Invdec around—6 sts.

- Fasten off with a slip stitch
into the next sc and leave
a long tail. Weave yarn tail
through the last round of
stitches, and pull tight to
close the hole. Sew body to
head. Weave in ends.

Regular Standard Body

The Regular Standard Body is for a dog that is medium-sized all
around. Great for Labrador Retrievers to Huskies (shown on page 45)
and everything in between, this pattern fits a wide range of dog body
types and breeds. An included pattern for a neck can be shortened or
extended, depending on the look you are going for.

Skill Level:
INTERMEDIATE

INSTRUCTIONS

Rnd 1: Starting at front end
of body, make an adjustable
ring, ch 1, work 6 sc into
ring. Pull closed—6 sts.
Insert a stitch marker into
the loop on your hook. Each
time you come back around
to the stitch marker, move it
up to the loop on your hook
to begin the next round.

Rnd 2: 2 sc into each st
around—12 sts.

MATERIALS AND TOOLS

Lightweight yarn in the fur
color(s) of your choice
(refer to page 159 for a list
of recommended yarns) **(3)**

Crochet hook: 2.75 mm
(size C-2 U.S.)

Stitch marker

Yarn needle

Polyester fiberfill stuffing

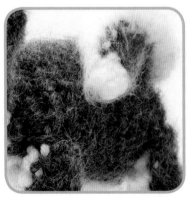

Rnd 3: *2 sc into next st, sc into next st; rep from * to end of rnd—18 sts.

Rnd 4: *2 sc into next st, sc into next 2 sts; rep from * to end of rnd—24 sts.

Rnd 5: *2 sc into next st, sc into next 7 sts; rep from * to end of rnd—27 sts.

Rnds 6–7: Sc into each st.

Rnd 8: *Invdec, sc into next 7 sts; rep from * to end of rnd—24 sts.

Rnds 9–10: Sc into each st.

Rnd 11: *Invdec, sc into next 6 sts; rep from * to end of rnd—21 sts.

Rnd 12: Sc into each st.

Rnd 13: *2 sc into next st, sc into next 6 sts; rep from * to end of rnd—24 sts.

Rnd 14: Sc into each st.

Rnd 15: *Invdec, sc into next 2 sts; rep from * to end of rnd—18 sts.

Rnd 16: Sc into each st.

- Insert stitch marker to hold your place and stuff body firmly.

Rnd 17: *Invdec, sc into next st; rep from * to end of rnd—12 sts.

Rnd 18: Invdec around—6 sts.

- Fasten off with a slip stitch into the next sc, and leave a long tail. Weave yarn tail through the last round of stitches, and pull tight to close the hole. Sew body to head unless creating a neck (see below). Weave in ends.

Neck (Optional):

Rnd 1: Ch 18, join in a ring with a sl st into first ch, and sc into each st around—18 sts.

Rnd 2: Sc into each st.

- Fasten off and leave a long tail for sewing. Sew ring of stitches to front of body, angled slightly, with yarn tail. Sew head to neck. No stuffing of the neck is necessary. Weave in ends.

Small Extended Body

We all know a doggy that has a long skinny body, like a Dachshund (shown below). The adorable way they carry themselves and their short little legs make them all the more cute.

Skill Level:
INTERMEDIATE

INSTRUCTIONS

Rnd 1: Starting at front end of body, make an adjustable ring, ch 1, work 6 sc into ring. Pull closed—6 sts. Insert a stitch marker into the loop on your hook. Each time you come back around to the stitch marker, move it up to the loop on your hook to begin the next round.

Rnd 2: 2 sc into each st around—12 sts.

Rnd 3: *2 sc into next st, sc into next st; rep from * to end of rnd—18 sts.

Rnds 4–15: Sc into each st.

Rnd 16: *Invdec, sc into next 4 sts; rep from * to end of rnd—15 sts.

Rnd 17: Sc into each st around.

Rnd 18: *Invdec, sc into next 3 sts; rep from * to end of rnd—12 sts.

- Insert a stitch marker to hold your place. Stuff body firmly.

Rnd 19: Invdec around— 6 sts.

- Fasten off with a slip stitch into the next sc, and leave a long tail. Weave yarn tail through the last round of stitches, and pull tight to close the hole. Sew body to head. Weave in ends.

MATERIALS AND TOOLS

Lightweight yarn in the fur color(s) of your choice (refer to page 159 for a list of recommended yarns) **(3)**

Crochet hook: 2.75 mm (size C-2 U.S.)

Stitch marker

Yarn needle

Polyester fiberfill stuffing

STITCHES AND TECHNIQUES USED

Adjustable ring, page 8

Chain (ch), page 6

Single crochet (sc), page 7

Invisible decrease (invdec), page 12

Slip stitch (sl st), page 7

(Optional) Changing color, page 14

Regular Extended Body

Weenie dogs aren't the only canines with long bodies! Corgis, Basset Hounds (shown below and on page 48), and other such breeds also have extended bodies that you'll want to use this regular size for. I've included an optional neck for this pattern because of the extended length of the body. It helps mark the head and body separation.

Skill Level:
INTERMEDIATE

INSTRUCTIONS

Rnd 1: Starting at front end of body, make an adjustable ring, ch 1, work 6 sc into ring. Pull closed—6 sts. Insert a stitch marker into the loop on your hook. Each time you come back around to the stitch marker, move it up to the loop on your hook to begin the next round.

Rnd 2: 2 sc into each st around—12 sts.

Rnd 3: *2 sc into next st, sc into next st; rep from * to end of rnd—18 sts.

Rnd 4: *2 sc into next st, sc into next 2 sts; rep from * to end of rnd—24 sts.

Rnd 5: *2 sc into next st, sc into next 7 sts; rep from * to end of rnd—27 sts.

Rnds 6–11: Sc into each st.

Rnd 12: *Invdec, sc into next 7 sts; rep from * to end of rnd—24 sts.

Rnds 13–17: Sc into each st.

Rnd 18: *Invdec, sc into next 6 sts; rep from * to end of rnd—21 sts.

Rnd 19: Sc into each st.

Rnd 20: *2 sc into next st, sc into next 6 sts; rep from * to end of rnd—24 sts.

Rnd 21: *Invdec, sc into next 2 sts; rep from * to end of rnd—18 sts.

MATERIALS AND TOOLS

Lightweight yarn in the fur color(s) of your choice (refer to page 159 for a list of recommended yarns)

Crochet hook: 2.75 mm (size C-2 U.S.)

Stitch marker

Yarn needle

Polyester fiberfill stuffing

STITCHES AND TECHNIQUES USED

Adjustable ring, page 8

Chain (ch), page 6

Single crochet (sc), page 7

Invisible decrease (invdec), page 12

Slip stitch (sl st), page 7

(Optional) Changing color, page 14

- Insert stitch marker to hold your place, and stuff body firmly.

Rnd 22: *Invdec, sc into next st; rep from * to end of rnd—12 sts.

Rnd 23: Invdec around—6 sts.

- Fasten off with a slip stitch into the next sc, and leave a long tail. Weave yarn tail through the last round of stitches, and pull tight to close the hole. Sew body to head unless creating a neck (see below). Weave in ends.

Neck (Optional):

Rnd 1: Ch 20, join in a ring with a sl st into first ch, and sc into each st around—20 sts.

- Fasten off and leave a long tail for sewing. Sew ring of stitches to front of body, angled slightly, with yarn tail. Sew head to neck. No stuffing of the neck is necessary. Weave in ends.

legs

Dog legs get our pets around, from food bowl to couch, to backyard for a good run, to bounding toward the front door when we get home. When they're puppies, their legs and feet grow faster than the rest of them do. Their sweet doggy paws are part of their charm.

From short and thick to long and slim, the next section will show you how to further complete your dog by adding four legs. Each pattern contains separate instructions for front legs and hind legs. Choose the legs that match your dog most closely. All patterns, Thick, Standard, and Thin, have short and long versions.

Short Thick Legs

We all know those small, stubby-legged dogs, like French Bulldogs, Corgis (shown on page 52), and Basset Hounds. Their short little legs work great with this pattern. Create two front legs and two hind legs. You'll finish up by stitching toe separations on each paw.

INSTRUCTIONS

Front Leg (Make 2):

Rnd 1: Starting at the paw of the leg, make an adjustable ring, ch 1, and work 9 sc into ring. Pull closed—9 sts. Insert a stitch marker into the loop on your hook. Each time you come back around to the stitch marker, move it up to the loop on your hook to begin the next round.

Rnds 2–3: Sc into each st around—9 sts.

Rnd 4: Invdec, sc into each st around—8 sts.

Rnd 5: *2 sc into next st, sc into next 3 sts; rep from * to end of rnd—10 sts.

Rnds 6–9: Sc into each st around.

Rnd 10: Sc in next 4 sts, 2 hdc in next st, hdc in next st, 2 hdc in next st, sc into next 3 sts—12 sts.

- Fasten off with a slip stitch into the next st, and leave a long tail. Stuff foot and leg, flattening top end slightly, and sew to side of body near the front. The longer sts from Rnd 10 should be on the outside of the body. Repeat for second leg, aligning the long sts from Rnd 10 on the outside of the other side of the body. Bend each leg slightly at the bottom for paws.

Hind Leg (Make 2):

Rnd 1: Starting at the paw of the leg, make an adjustable ring, ch 1, and work 9 sc into ring. Pull closed—9 sts. Insert a stitch marker into the loop on your hook. Each time you come back around to the stitch marker, move it up to the loop on your hook to begin the next round.

Rnds 2–3: Sc into each st around—9 sts.

Rnd 4: Invdec, sc into each st around—8 sts.

Rnd 5: *2 sc into next st, sc into next 3 sts; rep from * to end of rnd—10 sts.

Rnd 6: *2 sc into next st, sc into next 4 sts; rep from * to end of rnd—12 sts.

MATERIALS AND TOOLS

Lightweight yarn in the fur color(s) of your choice (refer to page 159 for a list of recommended yarns) **(3)**

Black embroidery floss

Crochet hook: 2.75 mm (size C-2 U.S.)

Stitch marker

Yarn needle

Embroidery needle

Polyester fiberfill stuffing

STITCHES AND TECHNIQUES USED

Adjustable ring, page 8

Chain (ch), page 6

Single crochet (sc), page 7

Invisible decrease (invdec), page 12

Half double crochet (hdc), page 9

Slip stitch (sl st), page 7

(Optional) Changing color, page 14

Rnd 7: *2 sc into next st, sc into next 5 sts; rep from * to end of rnd—14 sts.

Rnds 8–9: Sc into each st.

Rnd 10: Invdec, sc into next 5 sts, invdec, 2 hdc in next st, hdc in next 4 sts—13 sts.

- Fasten off with a slip stitch into the next s,t and leave a long tail. Stuff foot and leg, flattening top end slightly, and sew to side of body near the rear. The longer sts from Rnd 10 should be on the outside of the body. Repeat for second leg. Bend each leg slightly at the bottom for paws.

Finishing:

- With black embroidery floss and an embroidery needle, embroider three short straight stitches on each paw for toes.

Regular Thick Legs

Whether your larger dog is muscular or just carrying a few extra pounds, you'll probably want to use this pattern for Regular Thick Legs. Create two front legs and two hind legs. Stitch toe separations on each paw.

Skill Level:
INTERMEDIATE

INSTRUCTIONS

Front Leg (Make 2):

Rnd 1: Starting at the paw of the leg, make an adjustable ring, ch 1, and work 10 sc into ring. Pull closed—10 sts. Insert a stitch marker into the loop on your hook. Each time you come back around to the stitch marker, move it up to the loop on your hook to begin the next round.

Rnd 2: Sc into each st around.

Rnd 3: 2 sc into next st, sc into next 9 sts—11 sts.

Rnd 4: Sc into each st around.

Rnd 5: Invdec, sc into each st around—10 sts.

MATERIALS AND TOOLS

Lightweight yarn in the fur color(s) of your choice (refer to page 159 for a list of recommended yarns) **(3)**

Black embroidery floss

Crochet hook: 2.75 mm (size C-2 U.S.)

Stitch marker

Yarn needle

Embroidery needle

Polyester fiberfill stuffing

STITCHES AND
TECHNIQUES USED

Adjustable ring, page 8

Chain (ch), page 6

Single crochet (sc), page 7

Invisible decrease (invdec),
page 12

Slip stitch (sl st), page 7

Half double crochet (hdc),
page 9

(Optional) Changing color,
page 14

Rnds 6–7: Sl st into next 4 sts, hdc into next 6 sts—10 sts.

Rnd 8: Sc into each st—10 sts.

Rnd 9: 2 sc into next st, sc into next 9 sts—11 sts.

Rnds 10–12: Sc into each st.

Rnd 13: 2 sc into next st, sc into next 10 sts—12 sts.

Rnd 14: *2 sc into next st, sc into next 3 sts; rep from * to end of rnd—15 sts.

Rnd 15: Sc into each st.

Rnd 16: *Invdec, sc into next 3 sts; rep from * to end of rnd—12 sts.

Rnd 17: *Invdec, sc into next 2 sts; rep from * to end of rnd—9 sts.

- Fasten off with a slip stitch into the next st, and leave a long tail. Stuff foot and leg, flattening top end slightly, and sew to side of body near the front. Repeat for second leg. Bend each leg slightly at the bottom for paws.

Hind Leg (Make 2):

Rnd 1: Starting at the paw of the leg, make an adjustable ring, ch 1, and work 10 sc into ring. Pull closed—10 sts. Insert a stitch marker into the loop on your hook. Each time you come back around to the stitch marker, move it up to the loop on your hook to begin the next round.

Rnd 2: Sc into each st around.

Rnd 3: 2 sc into next st, sc in each st around—11 sts.

Rnd 4: Invdec, sc into each st around—10 sts.

Rnds 5–6: Sl st into next 4 sts, hdc into next 6 sts—10 sts.

Rnd 7: Sc into each st around—10 sts.

Rnd 8: 2 sc into next st, sc in each st around—11 sts.

Rnds 9–10: Sc into each st.

Rnd 11: 2 sc into next st, sc in each st around—12 sts.

Rnd 12: *2 sc into next st, sc in next 3 sts; rep from * to end of rnd—15 sts.

Rnd 13: 2 sc into next st, sc in each st around—16 sts.

Rnd 14: Sc into each st.

Rnd 15: Invdec, sc into each st around—15 sts.

- Fasten off with a slip stitch into the next st, and leave a long tail. Stuff foot and leg, flattening top end slightly, and sew to side of body near the rear. Repeat for second leg. Bend each leg slightly at the bottom for paws.

Finishing:

- With black embroidery floss and an embroidery needle, embroider three short straight stitches on each paw for toes.

Short Standard Legs

The Short Standard Legs are best suited for a smaller dog with medium-sized legs, like a Pug, a Poodle, or a Beagle (shown below). Create two front legs and two hind legs. Stitch toe separations on each paw.

Skill Level:
INTERMEDIATE

INSTRUCTIONS

Front Leg (Make 2):

Rnd 1: Starting at the paw of the leg, make an adjustable ring, ch 1, and work 7 sc into ring. Pull closed—7 sts. Insert a stitch marker into the loop on your hook. Each time you come back around to the stitch marker, move it up to the loop on your hook to begin the next round.

Rnds 2–3: Sc into each st around.

Rnd 4: Invdec, sc into each st around—6 sts.

Rnd 5: Sc into each st around.

Rnd 6: 2 sc in next st, sc into each st—7 sts.

Rnds 7–9: Sc into each st.

Rnd 10: 2 sc in next st, sc into each st—8 sts.

Rnd 11: 2 sc in next st, sc into each st—9 sts.

- Fasten off with a slip stitch into the next st, and leave a long tail. Stuff foot and leg, flattening top end slightly, and sew to side of body near the front. Repeat for second leg. Bend each leg slightly at the bottom for paws.

Hind Leg (Make 2):

Rnd 1: Starting at the paw of the leg, make an adjustable ring, ch 1, and work 7 sc into ring. Pull closed—7 sts. Insert a stitch marker into the loop on your hook. Each time you come back around to the stitch marker, move it up to the loop on your hook to begin the next round.

Rnd 2: Sc into each st around.

Rnd 3: Invdec, sc into each st around—6 sts.

Rnd 4: Sc into each st around.

Rnd 5: 2 sc into next st, sc in each st around—7 sts.

Rnds 6–7: Sc into each st around.

Rnd 8: 2 sc into first st, sc in each st around—8 sts.

Rnd 9: 2 sc into first st, sc in each st around—9 sts.

Rnd 10: 2 sc into first st, sc in each st around—10 sts.

MATERIALS AND TOOLS

Lightweight yarn in the fur color(s) of your choice (refer to page 159 for a list of recommended yarns) (3)

Black embroidery floss

Crochet hook: 2.75 mm (size C-2 U.S.)

Stitch marker

Yarn needle

Embroidery needle

Polyester fiberfill stuffing

STITCHES AND TECHNIQUES USED

Adjustable ring, page 8

Chain (ch), page 6

Single crochet (sc), page 7

Invisible decrease (invdec), page 12

Slip stitch (sl st), page 7

(Optional) Changing color, page 14

Rnd 11: 2 sc in next st, sc in next 4 sts, skip remaining stitches.

- Fasten off with a slip stitch into the next st, and leave a long tail. Stuff foot and leg, flattening top end slightly, and sew to side of body near the rear. Rnd 11 should be sewn on outside of body. Repeat for second leg. Bend each leg slightly at the bottom for paws.

Finishing:

- With black embroidery floss and an embroidery needle, embroider three short straight stitches on each paw for toes.

Regular Standard Legs

The Regular Standard Legs will work great for any medium-size or large dog, like a Labrador Retriever (shown on page 56) or German Shepherd. Create two front legs and two hind legs. Stitch toe separations on each paw.

INSTRUCTIONS

Front Leg (Make 2):

Rnd 1: Starting at the paw of the leg, make an adjustable ring, ch 1, and work 7 sc into ring. Pull closed—7 sts. Insert a stitch marker into the loop on your hook. Each time you come back around to the stitch marker, move it up to the loop on your hook to begin the next round.

Rnds 2–3: Sc into each st around.

Rnd 4: Invdec, sc into each st around—6 sts.

Rnd 5: Sc into each st around.

Rnd 6: 2 sc in next st, sc into each st—7 sts.

Rnds 7–9: Sc into each st.

Rnd 10: 2 sc in next st, sc into each st—8 sts.

Rnd 11: 2 sc in next st, sc into each st—9 sts.

Rnds 12–14: Sc in each st.

- Fasten off with a slip stitch into the next st, and leave a long tail. Stuff foot and leg, flattening top end slightly, and sew to side of body near the front. Repeat for second leg. Bend each leg slightly at the bottom for paws.

Skill Level:
INTERMEDIATE

MATERIALS AND TOOLS

Lightweight yarn in the fur color(s) of your choice (refer to page 159 for a list of recommended yarns) ③

Black embroidery floss

Crochet hook: 2.75 mm (size C-2 U.S.)

Stitch marker

Yarn needle

Embroidery needle

Polyester fiberfill stuffing

(continued on page 56)

Hind Leg (Make 2):

Rnd 1: Starting at the paw of the leg, make an adjustable ring, ch 1, and work 7 sc into ring. Pull closed—7 sts. Insert a stitch marker into the loop on your hook. Each time you come back around to the stitch marker, move it up to the loop on your hook to begin the next round.

Rnd 2: Sc into each st around—7 sts.

Rnd 3: Invdec, sc into each st around—6 sts.

Rnd 4: Sc into each st around.

Rnd 5: 2 sc into next st, sc in each st around—7 sts.

Rnds 6–7: Sc into each st around.

Rnd 8: 2 sc into first st, sc in each st around—8 sts.

Rnd 9: 2 sc into first st, sc in each st around—9 sts.

Rnd 10: 2 sc into first st, sc in each st around—10 sts.

Rnd 11: 2 sc in next st, sc in each st around—11 sts.

Rnds 12–14: Sc in each st.

- Fasten off with a slip stitch into the next st, and leave a long tail. Stuff foot and leg, flattening top end slightly, and sew to side of body near the rear. Repeat for second leg. Bend each leg slightly at the bottom for paws.

Finishing:

- With black embroidery floss and an embroidery needle, embroider three short straight stitches on each paw for toes.

Short Thin Legs

Little Yorkshire Terriers (shown below and on page 58) and Dachshunds scamper around on tiny legs, and this pattern is what you need if you're going to recreate a crocheted version of a little dog with thin legs. They're narrow and need very little stuffing, but the tight stitching should make them sturdy enough to support the weight of the rest of the dog.

Skill Level:
INTERMEDIATE

INSTRUCTIONS

Front Leg (Make 2):

Rnd 1: Starting at the paw of the leg, make an adjustable ring, ch 1, and work 5 sc into ring. Pull closed—5 sts. Insert a stitch marker into the loop on your hook. Each time you come back around to the stitch marker, move it up to the loop on your hook to begin the next round.

Rnds 2–5: Sc into each st around.

Rnd 6: 2 sc in next st, sc into each st—6 sts.

Rnd 7: 2 sc in next st, sc into each st—7 sts.

- Fasten off with a slip stitch into the next st, and leave a long tail. Stuff foot and leg, flattening top end slightly, and sew to side of body near the front. Repeat for second leg. Bend each leg slightly at the bottom for paws.

Hind Leg (Make 2):

Rnd 1: Starting at the paw of the leg, make an adjustable ring, ch 1, and work 5 sc into ring. Pull closed—5 sts. Insert a stitch marker into the loop on your hook. Each time you come back around to the stitch marker, move it up to the loop on your hook to begin the next round.

Rnds 2–4: Sc into each st around—5 sts.

Rnd 5: 2 sc into next st, sc in each st around—6 sts.

Rnd 6: *2 sc into next st, sc into next 2 sts; rep from * to end of rnd—8 sts.

Rnd 7: 2 sc into next st, sc into each st around—9 sts.

- Fasten off with a slip stitch into the next st, and leave a long tail. Stuff foot and leg, flattening top end slightly, and sew to side of body near the rear. Repeat for second leg. Bend each leg slightly at the bottom for paws.

MATERIALS AND TOOLS

Lightweight yarn in the fur color(s) of your choice (refer to page 159 for a list of recommended yarns) (3)

Black embroidery floss

Crochet hook: 2.75 mm (size C-2 U.S.)

Stitch marker

Yarn needle

Embroidery needle

Polyester fiberfill stuffing

STITCHES AND TECHNIQUES USED

Adjustable ring, page 8

Chain (ch), page 6

Single crochet (sc), page 7

Slip stitch (sl st), page 7

(Optional) Changing color, page 14

Finishing:

- With black embroidery floss and an embroidery needle, embroider three short straight stitches on each paw for toes.

Regular Thin Legs

A thin dog with long gangly legs will need a set of crocheted Regular Thin Legs. A good choice for a thin Dalmatian (shown on page 59) or Greyhound, these legs are skinny and long.

Skill Level:
INTERMEDIATE

INSTRUCTIONS

Front Leg (Make 2):

Rnd 1: Starting at the paw of the leg, make an adjustable ring, ch 1, and work 5 sc into ring. Pull closed—5 sts. Insert a stitch marker into the loop on your hook. Each time you come back around to the stitch marker, move it up to the loop on your hook to begin the next round.

Rnds 2–5: Sc into each st around.

Rnd 6: 2 sc in next st, sc into each st—6 sts.

Rnd 7: 2 sc in next st, sc into each st—7 sts.

Rnds 8–12: Sc into each st.

- Fasten off with a slip stitch into the next st, and leave a long tail. Stuff foot and leg, flattening top end slightly, and sew to side of body near the front. Repeat for second leg. Bend each leg slightly at the bottom for paws.

Hind Leg (Make 2):

Rnd 1: Starting at the paw of the leg, make an adjustable ring, ch 1, and work 5 sc into ring. Pull closed—5 sts. Insert a stitch marker into the loop on your hook. Each time you come back around to the stitch marker, move it up to the loop on your hook to begin the next round.

MATERIALS AND TOOLS

Lightweight yarn in the fur color(s) of your choice (refer to page 159 for a list of recommended yarns) (3)

Black embroidery floss

Crochet hook: 2.75 mm (size C-2 U.S.)

Stitch marker

Yarn needle

Embroidery needle

Polyester fiberfill stuffing

(Optional) Black permanent marker

Adjustable ring, page 8

Chain (ch), page 6

Single crochet (sc), page 7

Slip stitch (sl st), page 7

Invisible decrease (invdec), page 12

(Optional) Changing color, page 14

Rnds 2–4: Sc into each st around—5 sts.

Rnd 5: 2 sc into next st, sc in each st around—6 sts.

Rnd 6: *2 sc into next st, sc into next 2 sts; rep from * to end of rnd—8 sts.

Rnd 7: 2 sc into next st, sc into each st around—9 sts.

Rnds 8–11: Sc into each st.

- Fasten off with a slip stitch into the next st, and leave a long tail. Stuff foot and leg, flattening top end slightly,

and sew to side of body near the rear. Repeat for second leg. Bend each leg slightly at the bottom for paws.

Finishing:

- With black embroidery floss and an embroidery needle, embroider three short straight stitches on each paw for toes.

- Add spots, if you'd like, with a permanent marker.

tails

From long skinny tails to short stumpy tails, our friends on four legs use their tails to show us how they're feeling. Tails are also used for balance, agility, and communication. Different breeds have different types of tails, so choosing a tail pattern for your dog will help bring out the personality of your crocheted pet. Many animal shelters use tail types to help identify breeds of adoptable animals.

The Otter tail, Whip Tail, Sickle Tail, Ring Tail, and Docked Tail are all laid out for you to choose from in the following pages, in both large and small variations. Choose an Otter Tail for your athletic Labrador, or a Curled Tail for your smug Pug. A dog with a short little tail like a Bulldog or Doberman will need a crocheted Docked Tail, and for those with long skinny tails, make a Whip Tail. Own a furry Husky? Make a Sickle Tail. If your dog has no tail at all, like some Corgis or Australian Shepherds, you can skip this section altogether.

These patterns are all very easy to customize. If your dog happens to have a much longer tail or much shorter tail than the pattern creates, simply add or subtract rounds from the pattern. You'll see that this last piece of the dog puzzle will add lots of personality and the perfect finishing touch to your AmiguruME pup.

Otter Tail

The Otter Tail is usually found in dogs that are good swimmers, like Labrador Retrievers or even German Shepherds (shown below). Sporting dogs use these thick tapered tails like rudders in the water. Extend the tail as shown by repeating the last round to the desired length. Follow the instructions included in the pattern below for making a smaller Otter Tail.

INSTRUCTIONS

Rnd 1: Starting at tip of tail, make an adjustable ring, ch 1, work 4 sc into ring. Pull closed—4 sts. Insert a stitch marker into the loop on your hook. Each time you come back around to the stitch marker, move it up to the loop on your hook to begin the next round.

Rnd 2: Sc into each st around.

Rnd 3: 2 sc into next st, sc into each st—5 sts.

Rnd 4: 2 sc into next st, sc into each st—6 sts.

Rnd 5: 2 sc into next st, sc into each st—7 sts.

Rnd 6: 2 sc into next st, sc into each st—8 sts.

Rnds 7–8: Sc into each st.

- For a longer Otter Tail, repeat Rnd 8 as desired.

Rnd 9: *Invdec, sc into 2 sts; rep from * to end of rnd—6 sts.

Rnd 10: Sc into each st.

- Fasten off with a slip stitch into the next sc, and leave a long tail. Insert stuffing into tail and sew to body.

MATERIALS AND TOOLS

Lightweight yarn in the fur color(s) of your choice (refer to page 159 for a list of recommended yarns) (3)

Crochet hook: 2.75 mm (size C-2 U.S.)

Stitch marker

Yarn needle

Polyester fiberfill stuffing

STITCHES AND TECHNIQUES USED

Adjustable ring, page 8

Chain (ch), page 6

Single crochet (sc), page 7

Invisible decrease (invdec), page 12

Slip stitch (sl st), page 7

(Optional) Changing color, page 14

Whip Tail

Whip Tails are the long and skinny variety you see on lots of dogs, like Greyhounds, Dalmatians, Chihuahuas (shown below), and Great Danes. They require no stuffing, and can be as long or as short as you'd like. The entire tail is the same number of stitches repeated in rounds, so continue for as long as your dog's tail needs to be.

Skill Level:
INTERMEDIATE

INSTRUCTIONS

Rnd 1: Starting at tip of tail, make an adjustable ring, ch 1, work 4 sc into ring. Pull closed—4 sts. Insert a stitch marker into the loop on your hook. Each time you come back around to the stitch marker, move it up to the loop on your hook to begin the next round.

Rnds 2–8: Sc into each st around.

- For a longer tail, continue repeating Rnd 2.

- Fasten off with a slip stitch into the next sc, and leave a long tail. Sew to body.

MATERIALS AND TOOLS

Lightweight yarn in the fur color(s) of your choice (refer to page 159 for a list of recommended yarns) (3)

Crochet hook: 2.75 mm (size C-2 U.S.)

Stitch marker

Yarn needle

STITCHES AND TECHNIQUES USED

Adjustable ring, page 8

Chain (ch), page 6

Single crochet (sc), page 7

Slip stitch (sl st), page 7

(Optional) Changing color, page 14

Sickle Tail

If your dog's tail is carried up high, curving over his back, he has a Sickle Tail. Characterized by a curl upward over the back in a semicircle, a Sickle Tail will be a great choice for lots of different dogs, from a Husky (shown below) to a Pomeranian. Below you'll find instructions for a small and a regular size Sickle Tail.

INSTRUCTIONS

Small Sickle Tail

Row 1: Ch 11. Sc in 2nd ch from hook, *invdec, sc in next st; rep from * to end of rnd—7 sts.

Fasten off and leave a long tail. Sew to body.

Regular Sickle Tail

Rnd 1: Starting at tip of tail, make an adjustable ring, ch 1, work 4 sc into ring. Pull closed—4 sts. Insert a stitch marker into the loop on your hook. Each time you come back around to the stitch marker, move it up to the loop on your hook to begin the next round.

Rnd 2: Sc into each st around.

Rnds 3–14: Sc in next 2 sts, hdc in next 2 sts—4 sts.

- For a longer tail, continue repeating Rnd 3.

- Fasten off with a slip stitch into the next sc, and leave a long tail. Stuff if desired. Sew to body.

MATERIALS AND TOOLS

Lightweight yarn in the fur color(s) of your choice (refer to page 159 for a list of recommended yarns) **3**

Crochet hook: 2.75 mm (size C-2 U.S.)

Stitch marker

Yarn needle

STITCHES AND TECHNIQUES USED

Chain (ch), page 6

Single crochet (sc), page 7

Invisible decrease (invdec), page 12

Adjustable ring, page 8

Half double crochet (hdc), page 9

Slip stitch (sl st), page 7

(Optional) Changing color, page 14

Curled Tail

The screwy tail you see on Shiba Inus (see below) and Pugs is the Curled Tail. Make either a small or regular size, both explained below, for a dog with a curly tail.

Skill Level:
INTERMEDIATE

INSTRUCTIONS

Small Curled Tail

Row 1: Ch 7. Work 3 sc into 2nd ch from hook and next 5 chs—18 sts.

- Fasten off and leave a long tail for sewing. The tail will naturally curl upon itself. Sew the base to the body.

Regular Curled Tail

Row 1: Ch 15. 2 sc in 2nd ch from hook, sc in next ch, *2 sc in next ch, sc in next ch; rep from * to end of row—21 sts.

- Fasten off and leave a long tail for sewing. The tail will naturally curl upon itself. Sew the base to the body.

MATERIALS AND TOOLS

Lightweight yarn in the fur color(s) of your choice (refer to page 159 for a list of recommended yarns) (3)

Crochet hook: 2.75 mm (size C-2 U.S.)

Stitch marker

Yarn needle

STITCHES AND TECHNIQUES USED

Chain (ch), page 6

Single crochet (sc), page 7

(Optional) Changing color, page 14

Docked Tail

Dogs with Docked Tails have either been born that way, or, very commonly in breeds like the Doberman, Schnauzer (shown below), or Cocker Spaniel, had their tails surgically shortened or removed. If you have a dog with a short stubby tail, docked surgically or naturally, this pattern, in either the small or regular size, will suit your crocheted pet.

Skill Level:
INTERMEDIATE

INSTRUCTIONS

Small Docked Tail

Rnd 1: Make an adjustable ring, ch 1, and sc 4 into ring. Pull tail to close starting ring. Insert a stitch marker into the loop on your hook. Each time you come back around to the stitch marker, move it up to the loop on your hook to begin the next round.

Rnds 2–3: Sc into each st around.

- Fasten off and leave a long tail for sewing. Stuff if desired and sew to body.

Regular Docked Tail

Rnd 1: Make an adjustable ring, ch 1, and sc 5 into ring. Pull tail to close starting ring. Insert a stitch marker into the loop on your hook. Each time you come back around to the stitch marker, move it up to the loop on your hook to begin the next round.

Rnds 2–4: Sc into each st around.

- Fasten off and leave a long tail for sewing. Stuff, if desired, and sew to body.

MATERIALS AND TOOLS

Lightweight yarn in the fur color(s) of your choice (refer to page 159 for a list of recommended yarns) (3)

Crochet hook: 2.75 mm (size C-2 U.S.)

Stitch marker

Yarn needle

(Optional) Polyester fiber stuffing

STITCHES AND TECHNIQUES USED

Adjustable ring, page 8

Chain (ch), page 6

Single crochet (sc), page 7

(Optional) Changing color, page 14

dog breed guide

Dog Breed	Head	Ear
CHIHUAHUA	Small Pointed	Large Pointed
POMERANIAN	Small Pointed	Small Pointed
POODLE (TOY)	Small Pointed	Floppy
PUG	Small Blocky	Rose
WESTIE	Small Standard	Small Pointed
DACHSHUND	Small Pointed	Floppy
BULLDOG	Large Blocky	Rose
SCHNAUZER	Small Standard	Small Pointed
BEAGLE	Small Standard	Floppy
BASSETT HOUND	Large Standard	Floppy
CORGI	Large Pointed	Large Pointed
LABRADOR RETRIEVER	Large Standard	Drop
GOLDEN RETRIEVER	Large Standard	Drop
GERMAN SHEPHERD	Large Pointed	Large Pointed
DALMATIAN	Large Standard	Drop
SHIBA INU	Small Standard	Small Pointed
HUSKY	Large Standard	Large Pointed
ST. BERNARD	Large Standard	Drop
YORKIE	Small Standard	Small Pointed
ROTTWEILER	Large Blocky	Drop

Body	Legs	Tail	Yarn Type	Page No.
Small Standard	Short Thin	Whip	Smooth	63
Small Standard	Short Thin	Sickle	Fuzzy	25, 26
Small Standard	Short Standard	Docked	Boucle/Curly	34
Small Stocky	Short Standard	Curled	Smooth	23, 35
Small Stocky	Short Standard	Docked	Furry	41
Small Extended	Short Thin	Whip	Smooth	46
Regular Stocky	Regular Thick	Docked	Smooth	36, 53
Small Standard	Short Standard	Docked	Furry	37, 39, 66
Small Standard	Short Standard	Whip	Smooth	54
Regular Extended	Short Thick	Whip	Smooth	47, 48
Regular Extended	Short Thick	Docked	Fuzzy	38, 52
Regular Standard	Regular Standard	Otter	Smooth	56
Regular Standard	Regular Standard	Otter	Furry	33
Regular Standard	Regular Standard	Otter	Fuzzy	27, 62
Regular Standard	Regular Thin	Whip	Smooth	30, 59
Small Stocky	Short Standard	Curled	Fuzzy	29, 65
Regular Standard	Regular Standard	Sickle	Fuzzy	45
Regular Stocky	Regular Thick	Otter	Furry	43
Small Standard	Short Thin	Whip	Smooth	44, 57, 58
Regular Stocky	Regular Thick	Docked	Smooth	24

Dog Breed	Head	Ear
GOLDENDOODLE	Large Standard	Drop
PUGGLE	Small Blocky	Drop
YORKIPOO	Small Standard	Small Pointed
CHIWEENIE	Small Pointed	Large Pointed
PIT BULL	Large Blocky	Rose
FRENCH BULLDOG	Small Blocky	Large Pointed
BOXER	Large Blocky	Drop or Large Pointed
SHIH TZU	Small Standard	Drop
GREAT DANE	Large Standard	Large Pointed
BOSTON TERRIER	Small Blocky	Large Pointed
GREYHOUND	Small Pointed	Rose

BREEDS!

Body	Legs	Tail	Yarn Type
Regular Standard	Regular Standard	Otter	Bouclé/Curly
Small Standard	Short Standard	Curled	Smooth
Small Extended	Short Thin	Whip	Bouclé/Curly
Small Extended	Short Thin	Whip	Smooth
Regular Stocky	Regular Thick	Whip	Smooth
Small Stocky	Short Standard	Docked	Smooth
Regular Standard	Regular Standard	Docked	Smooth
Small Standard	Short Standard	Curled	Furry
Large Standard	Regular Standard	Whip	Smooth
Small Standard	Short Standard	Docked	Smooth
Regular Standard	Regular Thin	Whip	Smooth

cats

Are you more of a cat person? Do the calm purrs of a kitty sitting in your lap or a cat's playful pouncing make you swoon? I happen to love dogs AND cats, and I know how sweet the love of a feline can be. They're more content to live parallel lives with their owners, but they are always important parts of their families.

Crocheting your cat is a perfect way to make a permanent keepsake of your favorite pet. The patterns to follow are separated by body part, much like the Dogs section. There are Head types, round, triangular, and square, as well as Body types. By combining different elements you should be able to duplicate your own unique cat.

First choose a head shape. Next you'll crochet ears. Choose a body type, which each include legs. The tail is last.

For a short-haired cat, leave the yarn as is. For a longer haired cat, aggressively brush each piece before assembling with a slicker brush, as described on pages 16 and 17. In each pattern, I've suggested cat eyes and noses, as well as sizes, but feel free to use your favorite colors and even change the sizes if you prefer. There is plenty of flexibility in these patterns, so you really should be able to make any cat you'd like!

heads

Cats are generally shaped pretty similarly, but if you look closely there are three main types of heads, which can usually tell you a lot about the cat's breeding.

Many cats, like the American or British Shorthair, have round heads. The pattern makes a cute basic cat head that is probably the most common.

Cats of Asian descent have more triangular-shaped heads. This narrower, thinner face is a good choice for a Siamese or Sphynx cat.

Many larger cats, like Maine Coons, have square-shaped heads. The pattern for this type of head makes a flatter, more squared head.

Round Head

The Round Head pattern makes a cat head that starts at the nose and gradually widens into a round shape. Many European cats like the Manx (shown on page 77) have very round heads, and this Round Head pattern would work great with these kinds of cats. The first few rounds can be a different color from the rest of the head if your cat has a different colored muzzle.

INSTRUCTIONS

Head:

Rnd 1: Starting at muzzle area of head, make an adjustable ring, ch 1, work 6 sc into ring. Pull closed—6 sts. Insert a stitch marker into the loop on your hook. Each time you come back around to the stitch marker, move it up to the loop on your hook to begin the next round.

Rnd 2: Work 2 sc into each st around—12 sts.

Rnd 3: Sc in next 4, hdc in next 4 sts, sc in next 4 sts—12 sts.

Rnd 4: Sl st into each st around.

- *Change color after Rnd 4 if desired.

Rnd 5: *2 sc into next st, sc into next st; rep from * to end of rnd—18 sts.

Rnd 6: *2 sc into next st, sc into next 2 sts; rep from * to end of rnd—24 sts.

Rnds 7–11: Sc into each st around.

Rnd 12: *Invdec, sc into next 2 sts; rep from * to end of rnd—18 sts.

Rnd 13: *Invdec, sc into next st; rep from * to end of rnd—12 sts.

Insert safety eyes between Rnds 8 and 9, 5 sts apart. Insert cat nose into Rnd 2, positioned between eyes. Stuff head firmly and continue.

Rnd 14: Invdec around—6 sts.

- Fasten off with a slip stitch into the next sc, and leave a very long tail. Weave yarn tail through the last round of stitches, and pull tight to close the hole. Weave tail through to back of the bottom of the head and clip.

Cheeks (Make 2):

- Make an adjustable ring, ch 1, sc 5 into the ring. Fasten off.

- Sew each cheek to the head on either side of the nose. Weave in ends.

MATERIALS AND TOOLS

Lightweight yarn in the fur color(s) of your choice (refer to page 159 for a list of recommended yarns) **③**

Crochet hook: 2.75 mm (size C-2 U.S.)

Stitch marker

Yarn needle

7.5-mm safety cat eyes, color of your choice

9.5-mm plastic animal nose

Polyester fiberfill stuffing

STITCHES AND TECHNIQUES USED

Adjustable ring, page 8

Chain (ch), page 6

Single crochet (sc), page 7

Half double crochet (hdc), page 9

Slip stitch (sl st), page 7

Invisible decrease (invdec), page 12

(Optional) Changing color, page 14

Finishing:

- With yarn and a yarn needle, stitch one or two straight stitches across the top of the eye for eyelids (optional).

- With black embroidery floss and an embroidery needle, stitch a straight line down from the nose; then stitch two short lines below each cheek for the mouth.

Triangular Head

The sleek look of cats like the Sphynx and Siamese (shown on page 78) have a lot to do with the angular shape of their heads. The Triangular Head starts at the lowest part of the head and angles up in an exaggerated triangle shape.

Skill Level:

INTERMEDIATE

INSTRUCTIONS

Head:

Rnd 1: Starting at chin of head, make an adjustable ring, ch 1, work 6 sc into ring. Pull closed—6 sts. Insert a stitch marker into the loop on your hook. Each time you come back around to the stitch marker, move it up to the loop on your hook to begin the next round.

Rnd 2: *2 sc into next st, sc into next 2 sts; rep from * to end of rnd—8 sts.

Rnd 3: *2 sc into next st, sc into next 3 sts; rep from * to end of rnd—10 sts.

MATERIALS AND TOOLS

Lightweight yarn in the fur color(s) of your choice (refer to page 159 for a list of recommended yarns) (3)

Crochet hook: 2.75 mm (size C-2 U.S.)

Stitch marker

Yarn needle

(continued on page 78)

7.5-mm safety cat eyes, color of your choice

9.5-mm plastic animal nose

Embroidery needle

Black embroidery floss

Polyester fiberfill stuffing

STITCHES AND
TECHNIQUES USED

Adjustable ring, page 8

Chain (ch), page 6

Single crochet (sc), page 7

Invisible decrease (invdec), page 12

Slip stitch (sl st), page 7

(Optional) Changing color, page 14

Half double crochet (hdc), page 9

Rnd 4: *2 sc into next st, sc into next 4 sts; rep from * to end of rnd—12 sts.

Rnd 5: *2 sc into next st, sc into next 5 sts; rep from * to end of rnd—14 sts.

Rnd 6: *2 sc into next st, sc into next 6 sts; rep from * to end of rnd—16 sts.

Rnd 7: *2 sc into next st, sc into next 3 sts; rep from * to end of rnd—20 sts.

Rnd 8: *2 sc into next st, sc into next 4 sts; rep from * to end of rnd—24 sts.

Rnds 9-11: Sc into each st around.

Rnd 12: *Invdec, sc into next 2 sts; rep from * to end of rnd—18 sts.

- Insert safety eyes between Rnds 9 and 10, 6 sts apart. Insert cat nose into Rnd 2, centered between eyes. Stuff head firmly and continue.

Rnd 13: *Invdec, sc into next st; rep from * to end of rnd—12 sts.

Rnd 14: Invdec around—6 sts.

- Fasten off with a slip stitch into the next sc, and leave a very long tail. Weave yarn tail through the last round of stitches, and pull tight to close the hole. Weave tail through to back of the bottom of the head and clip.

Cheeks (Make 2):

Rnd 1: Make an adjustable ring. Ch 2, hdc 6 in ring. Pull tail to close ring.

- Sew each cheek to the head on either side of the nose. Weave in ends.

Finishing:

- With yarn and a yarn needle, stitch one or two straight stitches across the top of the eye for eyelids (optional).

- With black embroidery floss and an embroidery needle, stitch a straight line down from the nose; then stitch two short lines below each cheek for the mouth.

Square Head

If your cat has a flatter face or a wider head, you'll want to make a Square Head. Maine Coons (shown below) have squared heads as do Persians. Insert less stuffing into the nose area for an exaggerated Persian face.

INSTRUCTIONS

Head:

Rnd 1: Starting at muzzle area of head, make an adjustable ring, ch 1, work 6 sc into ring. Pull closed—6 sts. Insert a stitch marker into the loop on your hook. Each time you come back around to the stitch marker, move it up to the loop on your hook to begin the next round.

Rnd 2: 2 sc into each st—12 sts.

Rnd 3: Sc into each st.

Rnd 4: Sl st into each st around.

* Change to another color after Rnd 4 if desired.

Rnd 5: 2 sc into each st—24 sts.

Rnd 6: *2 sc into next st, sc into next 6 sts, 2 sc into next st, sc into next 4 sts; rep from * to end of rnd—28 sts.

Rnds 7–11: Sc into each st.

Rnd 12: *Invdec, sc into next 5 sts; rep from * to end of rnd—24 sts.

Rnd 13: Invdec around—12 sts.

- Insert nose between starting ring and Rnd 2, and safety eyes between Rnds 4 and 5, 4 sts apart. Stuff head firmly and continue.

Rnd 14: Invdec around—6 sts.

- Fasten off with a slip stitch into the next sc, and leave a very long tail. Weave yarn tail through the last round of stitches, and pull tight to close the hole. Weave tail through to back of the bottom of the head and clip.

Cheeks (Make 2):

Rnd 1: Make an adjustable ring. Ch 1, sc 5 in ring. Pull tail to close ring.

- Sew each cheek to the head on either side of the nose. Weave in ends.

Finishing:

- With yarn and a yarn needle, stitch one or two straight stitches across the top of the eyes for eyelids (optional).

- With black embroidery floss and an embroidery needle, stitch a straight line down from the nose; then stitch two short lines below each cheek for the mouth.

Skill Level:
INTERMEDIATE

MATERIALS AND TOOLS

Lightweight yarn in the fur color(s) of your choice (refer to page 159 for a list of recommended yarns) (3)

Crochet hook: 2.75 mm (size C-2 U.S.)

Stitch marker

Yarn needle

Embroidery needle

Black embroidery floss

7.5-mm safety cat eyes, color of your choice

9.5-mm plastic animal nose

Polyester fiberfill stuffing

STITCHES AND TECHNIQUES USED

Adjustable ring, page 8

Chain (ch), page 6

Single crochet (sc), page 7

Slip stitch (sl st), page 7

Invisible decrease (invdec), page 12

(Optional) Changing color, page 14

ears

Cats' ears are very expressive. Some are very small, and some are very large. Many have long hair pointed at the tips of the ears, like Maine Coons. Depending on the size of your cat's ears, the Ear Pattern can be easily altered.

All Ears

The Ear Pattern is the same for every cat. What you choose is how long you crochet. Are they very small? Crochet fewer rounds. Are they larger? Complete the pattern as written or extend them even further. Insert a little powdered blush or a triangle of pink felt in the inside of the ear if desired.

◇◇◇◇◇◇

Skill Level:
INTERMEDIATE

◇◇◇◇◇◇

INSTRUCTIONS

Rnd 1: Starting at the tip of the ear, make an adjustable ring, ch 1, and work 4 sc into ring. Pull closed—4 sts. Insert a stitch marker into the loop on your hook. Each time you come back around to the stitch marker, move it up to the loop on your hook to begin the next round.

Rnd 2: *2 sc, sc into next st; rep from * to end of rnd—6 sts.

Rnd 3: *2 sc, sc into next 2 sts; rep from * to end of rnd—8 sts.

Rnd 4: 2 sc into next st, sc into each st around—9 sts.

Rnd 5: 2 sc into next st, sc into each st around—10 sts.

Note: For smaller ears, fasten off and leave a long tail. For medium-sized ears, continue with Rnds 6–7.

Rnd 6: 2 sc into next st, sc into each st around—11 sts.

Rnd 7: 2 sc into next st, sc into each st around—12 sts.

Note: For a longer ear, repeat Rnd 7 as many times as desired.

- Fasten off with a slip stitch into the next sc, and leave a long tail. Flatten ear and stitch to top of head with yarn needle and yarn tail. Repeat for second ear.

MATERIALS AND TOOLS

Lightweight yarn in the fur color(s) of your choice (refer to page 159 for a list of recommended yarns) **(3)**

Crochet hook: 2.75 mm (size C-2 U.S.)

Stitch marker

Yarn needle

STITCHES AND TECHNIQUES USED

Adjustable ring, page 8

Chain (ch), page 6

Single crochet (sc), page 7

Slip stitch (sl st), page 7

(Optional) Changing color, page 14

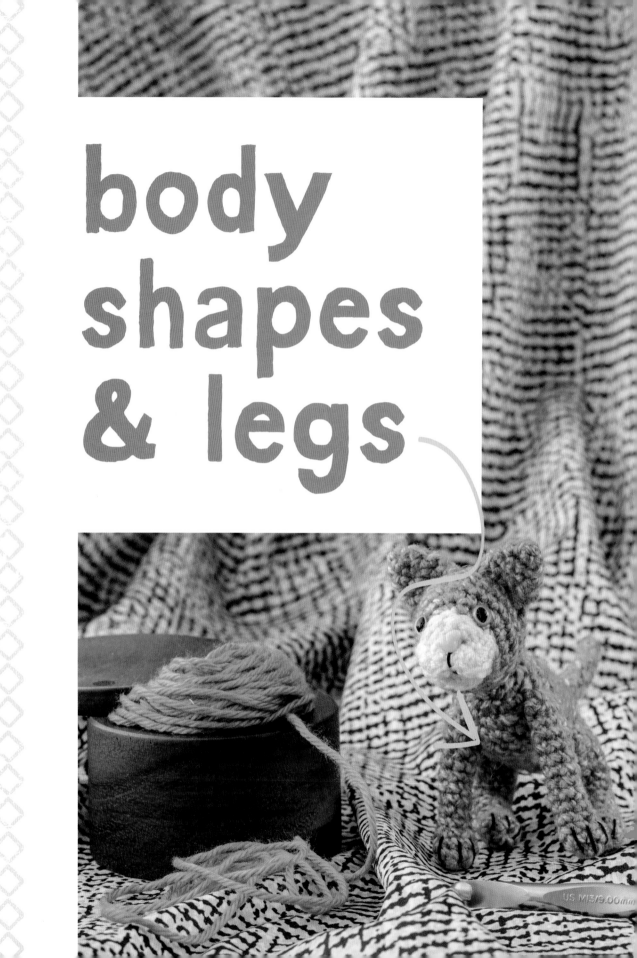

body
shapes
& legs

Do you have a fat cat? Is your cat long and lean? There are lots of different cat body types, and in the following pages I've written patterns for each of them.

If your cat is slim with thin legs, use the Slim Body pattern. It is great for a lanky Siamese cat.

If your cat is a standard size and medium all around, use the Medium Body pattern. The legs are a regular size and length, and the body should fit all medium-sized cats.

If your cat is larger or has a few extra pounds, crochet the Thick Body pattern. Even if your cat's extra fluff has more to do with fluffy hair than overeating, this pattern will create the right effect.

Each pattern includes instructions for a tail. Extend or shorten this pattern freely.

Remember to "fuzz up" your fur with a pet slicker brush. Brush each piece before assembling.

Slim Body and Legs

Sleek and slim, your cat has long legs and a narrow body. Crochet this pattern with smooth yarn.

INSTRUCTIONS

Body:

Rnd 1: Starting at front end of body, make an adjustable ring, ch 1, work 6 sc into ring. Pull closed—6 sts. Insert a stitch marker into the loop on your hook. Each time you come back around to the stitch marker, move it up to the loop on your hook to begin the next round.

Rnd 2: 2 sc into each st around—12 sts.

Rnd 3: *2 sc into next st, sc into next st; rep from * to end of rnd—18 sts.

Rnd 4: *2 sc into next st, sc into next 8 sts; rep from * to end of rnd—20 sts.

Rnds 5–8: Sc into each st.

Rnd 9: Invdec, sc into each st around—19 sts.

Rnds 10–12: Sc into each st around.

Rnd 13: Invdec, sc into each st around—18 sts.

Rnds 14–15: Sc into each st around.

Rnd 16: *2 sc into next st, sc into next 8 sts; rep from * to end of rnd—20 sts.

Rnd 17: *Invdec, sc into next 8 sts; rep from * to end of rnd—18 sts.

- Insert a stitch marker to hold your place. Stuff body firmly.

Rnd 18: *Invdec, sc into next st; rep from * to end of rnd—12 sts.

Rnd 19: Invdec around—6 sts.

- Fasten off with a slip stitch into the next sc, and leave a long tail. Weave yarn tail through the last round of stitches, and pull tight to close the hole. Weave in ends.

Front Legs (Make 2):

Rnd 1: Starting at paw end of leg, make an adjustable ring, ch 1, work 6 sc into ring. Pull closed—6 sts. Insert a stitch marker into the loop on your hook to hold your place as you continue.

Rnds 2–3: Sc into each st.

Rnd 4: Invdec, sc into each st around—5 sts.

Rnds 5–9: Sc into each st.

Rnd 10: 2 sc into next st, sc into each st around—6 sts.

Skill Level:
INTERMEDIATE

MATERIALS AND TOOLS

Lightweight yarn in the fur color(s) of your choice (refer to page 159 for a list of recommended yarns) (3)

Crochet hook: 2.75 mm (size C-2 U.S.)

Stitch marker

Yarn needle

Embroidery needle

Black embroidery floss

Polyester fiberfill stuffing

STITCHES AND TECHNIQUES USED

Adjustable ring, page 8

Chain (ch), page 6

Single crochet (sc), page 7

Invisible decrease (invdec), page 12

Slip stitch (sl st), page 7

Half double crochet (hdc), page 9

(Optional) Changing color, page 14

Rnds 11–12: Sc into each st.

Rnd 13: 2 sc into next st, sc into each st around—7 sts.

Row 14: Ch 1, turn, sl st into first st, sc into next 3 sts, sl st into next st. Leave remaining sts unworked—5 sts.

- Fasten off and leave a tail for sewing. Insert stuffing down into the paw and sparingly through the rest of the leg. Flatten the top of the leg, and sew to front side of the body, with Row 14 on the outside.

- Repeat for second front leg.

Hind Legs (Make 2):

Rnd 1: Starting at paw end of leg, make an adjustable ring, ch 1, work 6 sc into ring. Pull closed—6 sts. Insert stitch marker into the loop on your hook to hold your place as you continue. Move the marker up as you go.

Rnds 2–3: Sc into each st.

Rnd 4: Invdec, sc into each st around—5 sts.

Rnds 5–8: Sc into each st.

Rnd 9: 2 sc into next st, sc into each st around—6 sts.

Rnd 10: 2 sc into next st, sc into each st around—7 sts.

Rnd 11: 2 sc into next st, sc into each st around—8 sts.

Rnd 12: *2 sc into next st, sc into next 3 sts; rep from * to end of rnd—10 sts.

Rnds 13–14: Sc into each st around.

Row 15: Ch 1, turn, sl st into first st, sc into next st, hdc into next st, 2 hdc into next st, hdc into next st, sc into next st, sl st into next st. Leave remaining sts unworked—8 sts.

- Fasten off and leave a tail for sewing. Insert stuffing down into the paw and sparingly through the rest of the leg. Flatten the top of the leg, and sew to back side of the body, positioning Row 15 on the outside.

- Repeat for second hind leg.

Neck:

- The neck is optional and may be lengthened or shortened by adding or subtracting rounds.

Rnd 1: Ch 12. Sl st into first ch to form a ring. Sc into each st around—12 sts.

Rnd 2: Sc into each st.

- Fasten off and leave a long tail. Pin neck into place on top of front end of body at an angle. Stitch into place with yarn needle and yarn tail.

- With matching yarn, sew head to neck. Insert a little stuffing into the neck as you work the final stitches.

Tail:

Rnd 1: Make an adjustable ring, ch 1, sc 4 into ring. Pull closed—4 sts. Insert a stitch marker onto the loop on your hook to mark the beginning of the round. Move the marker up as you go.

Rnds 2–11: Sc into each st.

- Repeat Rnd 2 for a longer tail.

Rnd 12: 2 sc into next st, sc into each st—5 sts.

- Fasten off and leave a long tail. No stuffing is necessary. Sew tail to body and weave in ends.

Finishing:

- With black embroidery floss and embroidery needle, stitch three straight stitches on each paw for toes.

Medium Body and Legs

Most cats will probably fall into this category. From body shape to leg thickness, everything here is medium-sized.

MATERIALS AND TOOLS

Lightweight yarn in the fur color of your choice (refer to page 159 for a list of recommended yarns) (3)

Crochet hook: 2.75 mm (size C-2 U.S.)

Stitch marker

Yarn needle

Embroidery needle

Black embroidery floss

Polyester fiberfill stuffing

STITCHES AND TECHNIQUES USED

Adjustable ring, page 8

Chain (ch), page 6

Single crochet (sc), page 7

Invisible decrease (invdec), page 12

Slip stitch (sl st), page 7

(Optional) Changing color, page 14

INSTRUCTIONS

Body:

Rnd 1: Starting at front end of body, make an adjustable ring, ch 1, work 6 sc into ring. Pull closed—6 sts. Insert a stitch marker into the loop on your hook. Each time you come back around to the stitch marker, move it up to the loop on your hook to begin the next round.

Rnd 2: 2 sc into each st around—12 sts.

Rnd 3: *2 sc into next st, sc into next st; rep from * to end of rnd—18 sts.

Rnd 4: *2 sc into next st, sc into next 5 sts; rep from * to end of rnd—21 sts.

Rnds 5–11: Sc into each st.

Rnd 12: Invdec, sc into each st around—20 sts.

Rnds 13–16: Sc into each st around.

Rnd 17: Invdec around—10 sts.

- Insert a stitch marker to hold your place. Stuff body firmly.

Rnd 18: Invdec around—5 sts.

- Fasten off with a slip stitch into the next sc, and leave a long tail. Weave yarn tail through the last round of stitches, and pull tight to close the hole. Weave in ends.

Front Legs (Make 2):

Rnd 1: Starting at paw end of leg, make an adjustable ring, ch 1, work 7 sc into ring. Pull closed—7 sts. Insert a stitch marker into the loop on your hook to hold your place as you continue.

Rnds 2–3: Sc into each st.

Rnd 4: Invdec, sc into each st around—6 sts.

Rnds 5–9: Sc into each st.

Rnd 10: 2 sc into next st, sc into each st around—7 sts.

Rnd 11: Sc into each st.

Rnd 12: 2 sc into next st, sc into each st around—8 sts.

Row 13: Ch 1, turn, sl st into first st, sc into next 3 sts, sl st into next st. Leave remaining sts unworked—5 sts.

- Fasten off and leave a tail for sewing. Insert stuffing down into the paw and sparingly through the rest of the leg. Flatten the top of the leg, and sew to front side of the body, with Row 13 on the outside.

- Repeat for second front leg.

Hind Legs (Make 2):

Rnd 1: Starting at paw end of leg, make an adjustable ring, ch 1, work 7 sc into ring. Pull closed—7 sts. Insert stitch marker into the loop on your hook to hold your place as you continue. Move the marker up as you go.

Rnds 2–3: Sc into each st.

Rnd 4: Invdec, sc into each st around—6 sts.

Rnds 5–8: Sc into each st.

Rnd 9: 2 sc into next st, sc into each st around—7 sts.

Rnd 10: 2 sc into next st, sc into each st around—8 sts.

Rnd 11: *2 sc into next st, sc into next 3 sts; rep from * to end of rnd—10 sts.

Rnd 12: *2 sc into next st, sc into next 4 sts; rep from * to end of rnd—12 sts.

Rnds 13–14: Sc into each st around.

- Fasten off and leave a tail for sewing. Insert stuffing down into the paw and sparingly through the rest of the leg. Flatten the top of the leg, and sew to back side of the body.

- Repeat for second hind leg.

Neck:

- The neck is optional and may be lengthened or shortened by adding or subtracting rounds.

Rnd 1: Ch 13. Sl st into first ch to form a ring. Sc into each st around—13 sts.

Rnd 2: Sc into each st.

- Fasten off and leave a long tail. Pin neck into place on top of front end of body at an angle. Stitch into place with yarn needle and yarn tail.

- With matching yarn, sew head to neck. Insert a little stuffing into the neck as you work the final stitches.

Tail:

Rnd 1: Make an adjustable ring, ch 1, sc 4 into ring. Pull closed—4 sts. Insert a stitch marker onto the loop on your hook to mark the beginning of the round. Move the marker up as you go.

Rnds 2–11: Sc into each st.

- Repeat Rnd 2 for a longer tail.

Rnd 12: 2 sc into next st, sc into each st—5 sts.

- Fasten off and leave a long tail. No stuffing is necessary. Sew tail to body and weave in ends.

Finishing:

- With black embroidery floss and embroidery needle, stitch three straight stitches on each paw for toes.

Thick Body and Legs

Fluffy cats like the Persian (shown below and on page 89) will need the pattern for a Thick Body cat. The legs are slightly thicker, and the overall body shape is larger.

INSTRUCTIONS

Body:

Rnd 1: Starting at front end of body, make an adjustable ring, ch 1, work 6 sc into ring. Pull closed—6 sts. Insert a stitch marker into the loop on your hook. Each time you come back around to the stitch marker, move it up to the loop on your hook to begin the next round.

Rnd 2: 2 sc into each st around—12 sts.

Rnd 3: *2 sc into next st, sc into next st; rep from * to end of rnd—18 sts.

Rnd 4: *2 sc into next st, sc into next 2 sts; rep from * to end of rnd—24 sts.

Rnds 5–9: Sc into each st.

Rnd 10: Invdec, sc into each st around—23 sts.

Rnds 11–13: Sc into each st around.

Rnd 14: Invdec, sc into each st around—22 sts.

Rnds 15–16: Sc into each st around.

Rnd 17: Invdec around—11 sts.

- Insert a stitch marker to hold your place. Stuff body firmly.

Rnd 18: Sc into next st, invdec 5 times—6 sts.

- Fasten off with a slip stitch into the next sc, and leave a long tail. Weave yarn tail through the last round of stitches, and pull tight to close the hole. Weave in ends.

Front Legs (Make 2):

Rnd 1: Starting at paw end of leg, make an adjustable ring, ch 1, work 8 sc into ring. Pull closed—8 sts. Insert a stitch marker into the loop on your hook to hold your place as you continue. Move the marker up as you go.

Rnds 2–3: Sc into each st.

Rnd 4: Invdec, sc into each st around—7 sts.

Rnds 5–9: Sc into each st.

Rnd 10: 2 sc into next st, sc into each st around—8 sts.

MATERIALS AND TOOLS

Lightweight yarn in the fur color(s) of your choice (refer to page 159 for a list of recommended yarns) (3)

Crochet hook: 2.75 mm (size C-2 U.S.)

Stitch marker

Yarn needle

Embroidery needle

Black embroidery floss

Polyester fiberfill stuffing

STITCHES AND TECHNIQUES USED

Adjustable ring, page 8

Chain (ch), page 6

Single crochet (sc), page 7

Invisible decrease (invdec), page 12

Slip stitch (sl st), page 7

Half double crochet (hdc), page 9

(Optional) Changing color, page 14

Rnd 11: Sc into each st.

Rnd 12: 2 sc into next st, sc into each st around—9 sts.

Row 13: Ch 1, turn, sl st into first st, sc into next 3 sts, sl st into next st. Leave remaining sts unworked—5 sts.

- Fasten off and leave a tail for sewing. Insert stuffing down into the paw and sparingly through the rest of the leg. Flatten the top of the leg, and sew to front side of the body, with Row 13 on the outside.

- Repeat for second front leg.

Hind Legs (Make 2):

Rnd 1: Starting at paw end of leg, make an adjustable ring, ch 1, work 8 sc into ring. Pull closed—8 sts. Insert stitch marker into the loop on your hook to hold your place as you continue. Move the marker up as you go.

Rnds 2–3: Sc into each st.

Rnd 4: Invdec, sc into each st around—7 sts.

Rnds 5–8: Sc into each st.

Rnd 9: 2 sc into next st, sc into each st around—8 sts.

Rnd 10: *2 sc into next st, sc into next 3 sts; rep from * to end of rnd—10 sts.

Rnd 11: *2 sc into next st, sc into next 4 sts; rep from * to end of rnd—12 sts.

Rnd 12: *2 sc into next st, sc into next 5 sts; rep from * to end of rnd—14 sts.

Rnds 13–14: Sc into each st around.

- Fasten off and leave a tail for sewing. Insert stuffing down into the paw and sparingly through the rest of the leg. Flatten the top of the leg, and sew to back side of the body.

Neck:

- The neck is optional and may be lengthened or shortened by adding or subtracting rounds.

Rnd 1: Ch 15. Sl st into first ch to form a ring. Sc into each st around—15 sts.

Rnd 2: Sc into each st.

- Fasten off and leave a long tail. Pin neck into place on top of front end of body at an angle. Stitch into place with yarn needle and yarn tail.

- With matching yarn, sew head to neck. Insert a little stuffing into the neck as you work the final stitches.

Tail:

Rnd 1: Make an adjustable ring, ch 1, sc 4 into ring. Pull closed—4 sts. Insert a stitch marker onto the loop on your hook to mark the beginning

of the round. Move the marker up as you go.

Rnds 2–11: Sc into each st.

- Repeat Rnd 2 for a longer tail.

Rnd 12: 2 sc into next st, sc into each st—5 sts.

- Fasten off and leave a long tail. No stuffing is necessary. Sew tail to body and weave in ends.

Finishing:

- With black embroidery floss and embroidery needle, stitch three straight stitches on each paw for toes.

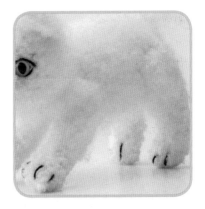

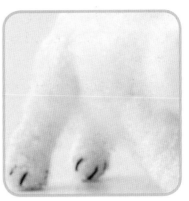

cat breed guide

Cat Breed	Head	Ear	Body & Legs	Tail	Yarn Type	Page No.
SPHYNX	Triangular	Large	Slim	Regular	Smooth	84, 85
SHORTHAIR	Round	Small	Medium	Regular	Furry	82, 86, 87
MAINE COON	Square	Large	Thick	Regular	Furry	79
PERSIAN	Square	Small	Thick	Regular	Furry	88, 89
SIAMESE	Triangular	Large	Slim	Regular	Smooth	78
MANX	Square	Small	Medium	No Tail	Furry	77

small
pets

Not everyone has a dog or a cat. Whether you want the quiet companionship of a bunny, a snake, or a fish, or the melodic friendship of a parakeet or parrot, small animals make great pets.

The animals in this section, being so small, take very little time to make. Lots of them use embroidered eyes and noses rather than plastic pieces, and you'll definitely save on yarn and stuffing since most of them use very little of either.

The same rules about choosing yarns will apply for Small Pets as we used in the Dogs and Cats patterns. If you're making a fuzzy bunny or guinea pig, use an acrylic or wool blend yarn and brush with a pet slicker brush if you'd like. A slithering snake or scaly fish can be made with a smooth cotton yarn.

These patterns are written as is, without interchangeable parts. That doesn't mean that you can't customize them. A simple change to the position of ears on the Rabbit will change it into lop-eared bunny, for example. Color changes will alter the look of the Guinea Pig or Parakeet. Spots added to the Pig pattern will turn it into your own prized pig.

rabbit

Besides dogs and cats, rabbits are one of the most popular pets. Use a soft yarn, and brush with a slicker brush if you'd like. Change colors at the tail for a white cotton-tailed bunny. The nose and mouth are stitched on with embroidery floss.

Head and Body:

Rnd 1: Starting at head, make an adjustable ring, ch 1, work 4 sc into ring. Pull closed—4 sts. Insert a stitch marker into the loop on your hook. Each time you come back around to the stitch marker, move it up to the loop on your hook to begin the next round.

Rnd 2: 2 sc into next st, sc into each st around—5 sts.

Rnd 3: 2 sc into next st, sc into each st around—6 sts.

Rnd 4: *2 sc into next st, sc into next st; rep from * to end of rnd—9 sts.

Rnd 5: 2 sc into each st—18 sts.

Rnd 6: *2 sc into next st, sc into next 8 sts; rep from * to end of rnd—20 sts.

Rnds 7–9: Sc into each st around.

Rnd 10: *Invdec, sc into next 8 sts; rep from * to end of rnd—18 sts.

Rnd 11: *Invdec, sc into next st; rep from * to end of rnd—12 sts.

Insert safety eyes between Rnds 5 and 6, 8 sts apart. Stuff head firmly and continue.

Rnd 12: *2 sc into next st, sc into next st; rep from * to end of rnd—18 sts.

Rnd 13: *2 sc into next st, sc into next 2 sts; rep from * to end of rnd—24 sts.

Rnds 14–17: Sc into each st.

Rnd 18: Invdec around—12 sts.

Rnd 19: Sc into each st.

- Hold place with a stitch marker, and stuff the head and body.

Rnd 20: Invdec around—6 sts.

- Change color for tail after Rnd 20 if desired.

Rnd 21: Ch 4, sc into 2nd ch from hook and next 2 sts, sl st into Rnd 20 (tail made).

- Fasten off with a slip stitch into the next sc, and leave a very long tail. Weave yarn tail through the last round of stitches, and pull tight to close the hole.

Front Legs (Make 2):

Rnd 1: Make an adjustable ring, ch 1, and sc 4 into the ring. Pull tail to close the hole—4 sts. Use a stitch marker to mark the beginning of the next round and to keep track of rounds.

Skill Level
INTERMEDIATE

MATERIALS AND TOOLS

Lightweight yarn in the fur color(s) of your choice (refer to page 159 for a list of recommended yarns) **3**

Crochet hook: 2.75 mm (size C-2 U.S.)

Stitch marker

Yarn needle

Embroidery needle

Black embroidery floss

5-mm safety eyes, color of your choice

Polyester fiberfill stuffing

STITCHES AND TECHNIQUES USED

Adjustable ring, page 8

Chain (ch), page 6

Single crochet (sc), page 7

Invisible decrease (invdec), page 12

Slip stitch (sl st), page 7

Half double crochet (hdc), page 9

(Optional) Changing color, page 14

Rnds 2–4: Sc into each st.

- Fasten off and leave a long tail for sewing. Sew each front leg to the side of the body. Weave in ends.

Hind Legs (Make 2):

Rnd 1: Make an adjustable ring, ch 1, and sc 6 into ring. Pull tail to close the hole— 6 sts.

Rnd 2: 2 sc into each st— 12 sts.

Rnds 3–4: Sc into each st.

Rnd 5: *Invdec, sc into next st; rep from * to end of rnd—8 sts.

Rnd 6: Invdec around—4 sts.

Rnds 7–9: Sc into each st.

- Fasten off and leave a long tail for sewing. Flatten the entire piece. No stuffing is necessary. Sew the rounded part of the leg to the side of the body, bending the narrow portion of Rnds 6–9 at a 45 degree angle, and stitch into place to simulate a rabbit's hind legs.

Ears (Make 2):

Row 1: Ch 7. Sc into 2nd ch from hook and next ch, hdc into next 4 chs.

Fasten off with a slip stitch into last ch. Leave a long tail for sewing.

- Stitch ear to side of head angled straight back. Weave in ends.

- Repeat for second ear.

Finishing:

- With black embroidery floss and an embroidery needle, stitch a v-shaped nose and small smile. If desired, use pink embroidery floss to fill in nose.

- With yarn and a yarn needle, stitch one or two straight stitches across the top of the eyes for eyelids (optional).

- Add a small bit of pink blush with your fingertip or a cotton swab to the inside of each ear (optional).

guinea pig

Guinea Pigs are generally easy to care for and make a good pet for someone with a small space. The pattern has lots of opportunity for personalization. Simple color changes go a long way to making the Guinea Pig look just like your own pet.

MATERIALS AND TOOLS

Lightweight yarn in the fur color of your choice (A) (refer to page 159 for a list of recommended yarns) (3)

Lightweight yarn in pink (B) (3)

Crochet hook: 2.75 mm (size C-2 U.S.)

Stitch marker

Yarn needle

Embroidery needle

Black embroidery floss

5-mm safety eyes, color of your choice

Polyester fiberfill stuffing

STITCHES AND TECHNIQUES USED

Adjustable ring, page 8

Chain (ch), page 6

Single crochet (sc), page 7

Invisible decrease (invdec), page 12

Slip stitch (sl st), page 7

Changing color, page 14

Head and Body:

Rnd 1: Starting at head with yarn A, make an adjustable ring, ch 1, work 4 sc into ring. Pull closed—4 sts. Insert a stitch marker into the loop on your hook. Each time you come back around to the stitch marker, move it up to the loop on your hook to begin the next round.

Rnd 2: 2 sc into each st around—8 sts.

Rnd 3: 2 sc into next st, sc into each st around—9 sts.

Rnd 4: 2 sc into each st—18 sts.

Rnds 5–6: Sc into each st.

Rnd 7: Invdec around—9 sts.

Rnd 8: 2 sc into each st around—18 sts.

Rnds 9–10: Sc into each st.

Rnd 11: *Invdec, sc into next 4 sts; rep from * to end of rnd—15 sts.

- Insert safety eyes between Rnds 3 and 4, 3 sts apart. Stuff head and body firmly and continue.

Rnd 12: *Invdec, sc into next 3 sts; rep from * to end of rnd—12 sts.

Rnd 13: Invdec around—6 sts.

- Fasten off with a slip stitch into the next sc. Weave yarn

tail through the last round of stitches, and pull tight to close the hole.

Legs (Make 4):

Row 1: With yarn B (pink), ch 3. Sc into 2nd ch from hook and next ch—2 sts.

- Fasten off and leave a long tail for sewing. Sew leg to underside of body.

- Repeat for remaining three legs.

Ears (Make 2):

Row 1: With yarn A, make an adjustable ring, ch 1, and sc 3 into ring—3 sts.

- Pull ring to close hole and fasten off.

- Stitch ear to side of head. Weave in ends.

- Repeat for second ear.

Finishing:

- With black embroidery floss and an embroidery needle, stitch a v-shaped nose and small smile. If desired, use pink embroidery floss to fill in nose.

- Add a small bit of pink blush with your fingertip or a cotton swab to the inside of each ear (optional).

mouse

Do you have a tiny mouse for a pet? Crochet this Mouse pattern in whatever color your little friend is, along with a little pink tail and nose.

MATERIALS AND TOOLS

Lightweight yarn in the fur color of your choice (A) (refer to page 159 for a list of recommended yarns) **(3)**

Lightweight yarn in pink (B) **(3)**

Crochet hook: 2.75 mm (size C-2 U.S.)

Stitch marker

Yarn needle

Black embroidery floss

Embroidery needle

Polyester fiberfill stuffing

STITCHES AND TECHNIQUES USED

Adjustable ring, page 8

Chain (ch), page 6

Single crochet (sc), page 7

Invisible decrease (invdec), page 12

Slip stitch (sl st), page 7

Half double crochet (hdc), page 9

(Optional) Changing color, page 14

INSTRUCTIONS

Head and Body:

Rnd 1: Starting at head with yarn A and C hook, make an adjustable ring, ch 1, work 4 sc into ring. Pull closed—4 sts. Insert a stitch marker into the loop on your hook. Each time you come back around to the stitch marker, move it up to the loop on your hook to begin the next round.

Rnd 2: 2 sc into each st around—8 sts.

Rnds 3–4: Sc into each st.

Rnd 5: *Invdec, sc into next 2 sts; rep from * to end of rnd—6 sts.

Rnd 6: *2 sc into next st, sc into next st; rep from * to end of rnd—9 sts.

Rnds 7–9: Sc into each st.

Rnd 10: Invdec, sc into each st around—8 sts.

Insert a stitch marker, and stuff head and body firmly.

Rnd 11: Invdec around—4 sts.

- Fasten off with a slip stitch into the next sc. Weave yarn tail through the last round of stitches, and pull tight to close the hole.

Legs (Make 4):

Row 1: With yarn B (pink), ch 2. Sc into 2nd ch from hook—1 st.

- Fasten off and leave a long tail for sewing. Sew each leg to underside of body.

Ears (Make 2):

Row 1: With yarn A, make an adjustable ring, ch 1, sc, hdc 2, sc into ring—4 sts. Pull ring to close hole and fasten off.

- Stitch ear to side of head. Weave in ends.

Tail:

Row 1: With pink yarn B, ch 9.

- Fasten off and weave in one end, and use other yarn tail to sew tail to body.

Finishing:

- With black embroidery floss and an embroidery needle, stitch a v-shaped nose and small smile. If desired, use pink embroidery floss to fill in nose.

- Stitch eyes with black embroidery floss, using a French knot.

- Add a small bit of pink blush with your fingertip or a cotton swab to the inside of each ear (optional).

hamster

Very similar to the Mouse pattern is this pattern for a Hamster. Many hamsters are furrier than their mice cousins, so brush this little guy with a slicker brush when you're done if you'd like. Add the tiny legs and embroider the face last.

MATERIALS AND TOOLS

Lightweight yarn in the fur color of your choice (A) (refer to page 159 for a list of recommended yarns) **3**

Crochet hook: 2.75 mm (size C-2 U.S.)

Stitch marker

Yarn needle

Black embroidery floss

Embroidery needle

Polyester fiberfill stuffing

STITCHES AND TECHNIQUES USED

Adjustable ring, page 8

Chain (ch), page 6

Single crochet (sc), page 7

Invisible decrease (invdec), page 12

Slip stitch (sl st), page 7

(Optional) Changing color, page 14

INSTRUCTIONS

Head and Body:

Rnd 1: Starting at head with yarn A, make an adjustable ring, ch 1, work 4 sc into ring. Pull closed—4 sts. Insert a stitch marker into the loop on your hook. Each time you come back around to the stitch marker, move it up to the loop on your hook to begin the next round.

Rnd 2: 2 sc into each st around—8 sts.

Rnds 3–4: Sc into each st.

Rnd 5: *Invdec, sc into next 2 sts; rep from * to end of rnd—6 sts.

Rnd 6: *2 sc into next st, sc into next st; rep from * to end of rnd—9 sts.

Rnds 7–9: Sc into each st.

Rnd 10: Invdec, sc into each st around—8 sts.

- *Insert a stitch marker, and stuff head and body firmly.

Rnd 11: Invdec around—4 sts.

- Fasten off with a slip stitch into the next sc. Weave yarn tail through the last round of stitches, and pull tight to close the hole.

Legs (Make 4):

Row 1: With yarn A, ch 2. Sc into 2nd ch from hook—1 st.

- Fasten off and leave a long tail for sewing. Sew leg to underside of body.

- Repeat three times for the remaining legs.

Ears (Make 2):

Row 1: With yarn A, ch 3, sl st into first ch. Fasten off.

- Stitch ear to side of head. Weave in ends.

- Repeat for second ear.

Finishing:

- With black embroidery floss and an embroidery needle, stitch a v-shaped nose and small smile. If desired, use pink embroidery floss to fill in nose.

- Stitch eyes with black embroidery floss, using a French knot.

- Add a small bit of pink blush with your fingertip or a cotton swab to the inside of each ear (optional).

parakeet

My bird-loving aunt had two parakeets named Waylon and Willie. Commonly, parakeets are blue or green, but choose whatever color you'd like for your pet. A pipe cleaner makes tiny legs and feet.

Skill Level
INTERMEDIATE

MATERIALS AND TOOLS

White lightweight yarn (A) (refer to page 159 for a list of recommended yarns)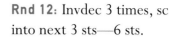

Pastel blue lightweight yarn (or color of your choice) (B)

Crochet hook: 2.75 mm (size C-2 U.S.)

Stitch marker

Yarn needle

Embroidery needle

Black embroidery floss

Yellow embroidery floss

Polyester fiberfill stuffing

Gray pipe cleaner

STITCHES AND TECHNIQUES USED

Adjustable ring, page 8

Chain (ch), page 6

Single crochet (sc), page 7

Invisible decrease (invdec), page 12

Half double crochet (hdc), page 9

Slip stitch (sl st), page 7

Double crochet (dc), page 10

Changing color, page 14

Head/Body:

Rnd 1: Starting at top of head with yarn A and C hook, make an adjustable ring, ch 1, work 6 sc into ring. Pull closed—6 sts. Insert a stitch marker into the loop on your hook. Each time you come back around to the stitch marker, move it up to the loop on your hook to begin the next round.

Rnds 2–4: Sc into each st around.

Change to yarn B at the end of Rnd 4.

Rnd 5: 2 sc into next st, sc into each st around—7 sts.

Rnd 6: 2 sc into next st, sc into each st around—8 sts.

Rnds 7–9: Sc into each st.

Rnd 10: 2 sc into next st, sc into each st around—9 sts.

Rnd 11: Sc into each st.

- Insert stitch marker to hold your place, and stuff head and body.

Rnd 12: Invdec 3 times, sc into next 3 sts—6 sts.

Row 13: Ch 6, sc into 2nd ch from hook and next ch, hdc into next 3 chs, sl st into next st (tail made)—6 sts.

- Fasten off and leave a long tail. Close up hole by weaving tail through the stitches in Rnd 12. Weave in ends.

Tail Feather:

Row 1: With yarn B, ch 9. Hdc into 3rd ch and each additional ch—7 sts.

- Fasten off and sew tail feather under the tail created in Row 13 of the head/body.

Wings (Make 2):

Row 1: With yarn A (white) and black embroidery floss held together, ch 6, sl st into 2nd ch from hook and next ch, hdc in next, dc in next, ch 2, sl st into last ch.

- Fasten off and sew wing to side of body.

- Repeat for second wing.

Finishing:

- With black embroidery floss and embroidery needle, stitch tiny straight horizontal stitches all around the back and sides of the head.

- With black embroidery floss, create eyes with two French knots one each on either side of the head.

- With yellow embroidery floss, stitch a beak on the front of the head.

- With yarn B and a yarn needle, stitch across the top of the beak.

- Fold the pipe cleaner in half and run through the bottom of the body. Bend the legs down and curl ends, cutting off excess, to form tiny feet.

parrot

These large birds are exotic and beautiful. They can be trained and make interesting and unique pets. The coloring in my example is for a red parrot, but you can change any of the recommendations to match your own pet.

Head/Body:

Rnd 1: Starting at top of head with yarn A, make an adjustable ring, ch 1, work 6 sc into ring. Pull closed—6 sts. Insert a stitch marker into the loop on your hook. Each time you come back around to the stitch marker, move it up to the loop on your hook to begin the next round.

Rnd 2: *2 sc into next st, sc into next st; rep from * to end of rnd—9 sts.

Rnds 3–5: Sc into each st around.

Rnd 6: 2 sc into next st, sc into each st around—10 sts.

Rnd 7: 2 sc into next st, sc into each st around—11 sts.

Rnd 8: 2 sc into next st, sc into each st around—12 sts.

Rnds 9–11: Sc into each st.

Rnd 12: 2 sc into next st, sc into each st around—13 sts.

Rnd 13: Sc into each st.

Rnd 14: 2 sc into next st, sc into each st around—14 sts.

Rnd 15: *Invdec, sc into next 5 sts; rep from * to end of rnd—12 sts.

- Insert stitch marker to hold your place, and stuff head and body.

Rnd 16: Invdec 4 times, sc into next 4 sts—8 sts.

Rnd 17: Invdec 2 times, sc in next 4 sts—6 sts.

Row 18: Ch 11, hdc into 3rd ch from hook and next 8 ch, sl st into next st (tail made)—9 sts.

- Fasten off and leave a long tail. Weave tail through the last round of stitches in Rnd 17 to close the hole. Weave in ends.

Tail Feathers (Make 2):

Row 1: With yarn B (blue), ch 11. Hdc into 3rd ch and each additional ch—9 sts.

- Fasten off and sew tail feather under the tail created in Row 18 of the head/body.

- Repeat for second tail feather.

Wings (Make 2):

Row 1: With yarn A (red) make an adjustable ring, ch 1, and sc 4 into ring—4 sts. Pull tail to close the hole. You will now work in rows along the edge of the semicircle just made.

Row 2: Ch 1, turn to work into edge of semicircle, sc 3 evenly—3 sts.

Skill Level
INTERMEDIATE

MATERIALS AND TOOLS

Red lightweight yarn (or color of your choice) (A) (refer to page 159 for a list of recommended yarns) (3)

Blue lightweight yarn (or color of your choice) (B) (3)

Yellow lightweight yarn (or color of your choice) (C) (3)

Crochet hook: 2.75 mm (size C-2 U.S.)

Stitch marker

Yarn needle

Embroidery needle

Black embroidery floss

White felt

Polyester fiberfill stuffing

Black pipe cleaner

(continued on page 108)

Adjustable ring, page 8

Chain (ch), page 6

Single crochet (sc), page 7

Invisible decrease (invdec), page 12

Half double crochet (hdc), page 9

Slip stitch (sl st), page 7

Changing color, page 14

Rows 3–4: Ch 1, turn, sc into each st—3 sts.

Change to yellow yarn C at the end of Row 4.

Row 5: Ch 1, turn, sc into each st.

Change to blue yarn B at the end of Row 5.

Rows 6–9: Ch 1, turn, sc into each st.

Row 10: Ch 1, turn, invdec, sc in next st—2 sts.

Row 11: Ch 1, turn, sc into each st.

Row 12: Ch 1, turn, invdec—1 st.

- Fasten off and sew wing to side of body. Weave in ends.

- Repeat for second wing.

Beak:

Rnd 1: With yarn C (yellow), make an adjustable

ring, ch 2, hdc 3 into ring. Fasten off and pull tail to close ring.

- Sew beak to face of parrot.

Finishing:

- Cut two small circles from white felt.

- With black embroidery floss, create eyes with two French knots into the center of each white felt circle. Glue or stitch circles to each side of the head.

- With black embroidery floss, stitch around the top of the beak.

- Fold the pipe cleaner in half and run through the bottom of the body. Bend the legs down and curl ends, cutting off excess, to form feet.

snake

Snakes may not be for everyone, but many pet owners enjoy the low-maintenance aspects and longevity of pet snakes. The Snake featured here resembles a Ball Python, but by changing the color and markings, you could make any snake you'd like. This pattern is easy to adapt into a longer snake. By starting with a longer chain, and thereby increasing the number of sc in each row, your snake will grow into whatever size you choose.

MATERIALS AND TOOLS

Lightweight yarn in the color of your choice (refer to page 159 for a list of recommended yarns) **3**

Crochet hook: 2.75 mm (size C-2 U.S.)

Stitch marker

Yarn needle

Embroidery needle

Black embroidery floss

Permanent markers (brown, black, etc. for markings)

Polyester fiberfill stuffing

STITCHES AND TECHNIQUES USED

Chain (ch), page 6

Slip stitch (sl st), page 7

Single crochet (sc), page 7

Half double crochet (hdc), page 9

Head/Body:

Row 1: Ch 39. Sl st into 2nd ch from hook, sc into next 32 chs, sl st into next ch, 2 hdc into next ch, sc in next ch, sl st into last ch—38 sts

Row 2: Ch 1, turn, sl st into first st , sc in next st, hdc in next 2 sts, sl st in next st, sc in next 32 sts, sl st in last st—38 sts.

Row 3: Ch 1, turn, sl st in first st, sc in next 32 sts, sl st in next st, hdc in next 2 sts, sc in next st, sl st in last st—38 sts.

Rows 4–5: Repeat Rows 2–3.

Row 6: Ch 1, turn, sl st in first st, sc in next st, hdc in next 2 sts, sc in next st, sl st in next st, leave remaining 33 sts unworked—5 sts.

Rows 7: Ch 1, turn, sl st in first st, hdc in next 2, sc in next st, sl st in last st—5 sts.

Rows 8: Ch 1, turn, sl st in first st, sc in next st, hdc in next 2, sl st in last st—5 sts.

- Fasten off and leave a very long tail for sewing.

- Using the yarn tail and a yarn needle, seam the entire length of the snake, adding stuffing if desired. The short Rows 6–8 should be sewn closed around each edge, creating the head. Weave in ends.

Finishing:

- With black embroidery floss and embroidery needle, stitch a French knot on each side of the head for eyes.

- As desired, mark the snake with the permanent markers in diamond or stripe patterns.

turtle

We had a turtle once named Speedy. This turtle looks just like him, a Red-eared Slider. Change the markings on the shell, head, and legs for a different look.

MATERIALS AND TOOLS

Dark green lightweight yarn (A) (refer to page 159 for a list of recommended yarns) **3**

Green lightweight yarn (B) **3**

Crochet hook: 2.75 mm (size C-2 U.S.)

Stitch marker

Yarn needle

Embroidery needle

Black, red, yellow, and brown embroidery floss

Polyester fiberfill stuffing

STITCHES AND TECHNIQUES USED

Chain (ch), page 6

Single crochet (sc), page 7

Front loops only (FLO), page 13

Invisible decrease (invdec), page 12

Adjustable ring, page 8

Half double crochet (hdc), page 9

Slip stitch (sl st), page 7

(Optional) Changing color, page 14

INSTRUCTIONS

Shell:

Rnd 1: With yarn A and C hook, ch 3. Sc into 2nd ch from hook, sc 5 in last sc, working into opposite side of ch, sc in next ch, sc 5 in last sc—12 sts.

Rnd 2: *2 sc in next st, sc in next 3 sts; rep from * to end of rnd—15 sts.

Rnd 3: *2 sc in next st, sc in next 4 sts; rep from * to end of rnd—18 sts.

Rnd 4: *2 sc in next st, sc in next 5 sts; rep from * to end of rnd—21 sts.

Rnd 5: Sc in each st around.

Rnd 6: Working in front loops only (FLO) of each st, *2 sc in next st, sc in next 2 sts: rep from * to end of rnd—28 sts.

- Fasten off and weave in ends.

Belly plate:

Row 1: With yarn A, ch 5. Sc in 2nd ch from hook and next 3 chs—4 sts.

Row 2: Ch 1, turn, 2 sc in first st, sc in next 2 sts, 2 sc in last ch—6 sts.

Rows 3–6: Ch 1, turn, sc in each st.

Row 7: Ch 1, turn, invdec, sc in next 2, invdec—4 sts.

Row 8: Ch 1, turn, sc in each st.

- Fasten off and leave a long tail. Sew belly plate to underside of shell, stuffing as you close up the last few stitches. Weave in ends.

Head:

Rnd 1: With yarn B, make an adjustable ring, ch 1, sc 6 into ring. Pull tail to close ring—6 sts.

Rnd 2: *2 sc in next st, sc in next 2 sts; rep from * to end of rnd—8 sts.

Rnds 3–4: Sc in each st.

Rnd 5: Invdec 3 times, sc in next 2 sts—5 sts.

- Fasten off and leave a long tail. Stuff head and sew under edge of shell. Weave in ends.

Feet (Make 4):

Row 1: With yarn B, ch 4. Hdc into 3rd ch from hook, sc in last ch—2 sts.

- Fasten off and sew under edge of shell. Weave in ends.

- Repeat three times for remaining feet.

Tail:

Row 1: With yarn B, ch 2. Sl st into 2nd ch from hook—1 st.

- Fasten off and leave a long tail for sewing. Sew tail under edge of shell. Weave in ends.

Finishing:

- With black embroidery floss and embroidery needle, stitch a French knot on each side of the head for eyes.

- With yellow embroidery floss and embroidery needle, stitch short straight stitches on head and feet for stripes.

- With red embroidery floss and embroidery needle, stitch a short straight stitch near each eye.

- With brown embroidery floss, stitch a checkered pattern around shell.

fish

Pet fish can turn into a fun and expensive hobby. This Fish pattern can be changed in all kinds of ways. To make a goldfish, crochet it all in orange. For a Betta, make it a couple of different colors. The Fish is really cute displayed in a tiny plastic bag, like he was just bought from a pet store!

Head/Body:

Rnd 1: Make an adjustable ring, ch 1, sc 4 into ring. Pull tail to close hole—4 sts.

Rnd 2: *2 sc in next st, sc in next st; rep from * to end of rnd—6 sts.

Rnd 3: *2 sc in next st, sc in next 2 sts; rep from * to end of rnd—8 sts.

Rnds 4–5: Sc in each st.

Rnd 6: Invdec around—4 sts.

Insert a tiny bit of stuffing into the fish if desired. Continue crocheting to create the tail.

Row 7: Ch 6, dc into 4th ch from hook, hdc in next 2 chs, sl st into next st, ch 6, dc into 4th ch from hook, hdc in next 2 sts, sl st in next st.

- Fasten off and leave a long tail. Weave tail through the stitches in Rnd 6 to close hole. Weave in ends.

Top/Bottom Fins (Make 2):

Row 1: Ch 5. Dc in 3rd ch from hook, hdc in next ch, sl st in last ch.

- Fasten off. Repeat for second fin, and sew fins to top edge and bottom edges of body.

Side Fins (Make 2):

Row 1: Ch 4. Dc in 3rd ch from hook, sc in next ch.

- Fasten off. Repeat for second fin, and sew each fin to one side of the body.

Finishing:

- With black embroidery floss and embroidery needle, stitch a French knot on each side of the head for eyes.

Skill Level
INTERMEDIATE

MATERIALS AND TOOLS

Lightweight yarn in the color of your choice (refer to page 159 for a list of recommended yarns) **(3)**

Crochet hook: 2.75 mm (size C-2 U.S.)

Stitch marker

Yarn needle

Embroidery needle

Black embroidery floss

Polyester fiberfill stuffing

STITCHES AND TECHNIQUES USED

Adjustable ring, page 8

Chain (ch), page 6

Single crochet (sc), page 7

Invisible decrease (invdec), page 12

Double crochet (dc), page 10

Half double crochet (hdc), page 9

Slip stitch (sl st), page 7

pig

Whether pot-bellied or mini, pet pigs are growing in popularity and are extremely adorable! This one is all pink, but add spots anywhere for the particular look you'd like. Pot-bellied pigs can be crocheted in dark gray. Don't forget to add some extra stuffing in the body!

Head/Body:

Rnd 1: Starting at back of body, make an adjustable ring, ch 1, sc 6 into ring. Pull tail to close hole—6 sts.

Rnd 2: *2 sc in each st—12 sts.

Rnd 3: *2 sc in first st, sc in next st—18 sts.

Rnds 4–11: Sc in each st.

Rnd 12: Invdec 3 times, sc in 12 sts—15 sts.

Rnd 13: Work 3 sc into next 3 sts, sc in next 12 sts—21 sts.

Rnd 14: Sc in 9 sts, *invdec, sc in next 2 sts; rep from * to end of rnd—18 sts.

Rnd 15: Sc in each st.

Rnd 16: *Invdec, sc in next 4 sts; rep from * to end of rnd—15 sts.

Rnd 17: *Invdec, sc in next 3 sts; rep from * to end of rnd—12 sts.

Rnd 18: Invdec 3 times, sc in next 6 sts—9 sts.

- Hold your place with a stitch marker, and insert safety eyes between Rnds 15 and 16, 6 sts apart. The top of the head is where the 3 invdec are positioned. Stuff body and head.

Rnd 19: Sc in next 6 sts, invdec, sc in next st—8 sts.

Rnd 20: Invdec, sc in next 6 sts—7 sts.

- Fasten off and leave a long tail. With a yarn needle stitch the last round closed, creating the pig snout. Weave in ends.

Legs (Make 4):

Rnd 1: Starting at the top of the leg, make an adjustable ring, ch 1, sc 5 into ring. Pull tail to close hole—5 sts.

Rnds 2–6: Sc into each st.

- Fasten off and leave a long tail. Insert stuffing if desired, and sew each leg to the body. Weave in ends.

- Repeat for remaining three legs.

Ears (Make 2):

Row 1: Ch 6. Sl st into 2nd ch from hook, hdc in next ch, dc in next 2 chs, ch 3, sl st into last ch.

- Fasten off and sew the ear to the side of the head.

- Repeat for the second ear.

Tail:

Row 1: Ch 6.

- Fasten off. Weave in starting yarn through ch.

- Sew tail to back end with yarn needle. Weave in ends.

Finishing:

- With black embroidery floss and embroidery needle, stitch two tiny stitches for nostrils, and one or two long stitches under the snout for the smile.

Skill Level
INTERMEDIATE

MATERIALS AND TOOLS

Lightweight yarn in the color of your choice (refer to page 159 for a list of recommended yarns) (3)

Crochet hook: 2.75 mm (size C-2 U.S.)

5-mm safety eyes

Stitch marker

Yarn needle

Embroidery needle

Black embroidery floss

Polyester fiberfill stuffing

STITCHES AND TECHNIQUES USED

Adjustable ring, page 8

Chain (ch), page 6

Single crochet (sc), page 7

Invisible decrease (invdec), page 12

Slip stitch (sl st), page 7

Half double crochet (hdc), page 9

Double crochet (dc), page 10

fantasy
pets

There are dog people and there are cat people, and there are hamster people and there are bird people. What about sloth people? Or unicorn people? What if you could have any pet you wanted? Truthfully, how cool would it be to have a precious little penguin waddling around your house or a bear cub sleeping at the foot of your bed?

Some of the animals in this section are attainable. There are people with pet monkeys, and there are lots of people with pet ponies. Most people aren't able to have them, but they're possible. Others are a little far-fetched, but these are fantasy pets. Crochet a pet T-rex for a dinosaur lover. How about a fox for someone with an affinity for those little woodland creatures? There's even a big green dragon!

Each of these patterns contains specific instructions, but feel free to alter any element you'd like. If you want an orange penguin, by all means, crochet your penguin with orange yarn. If you want your turquoise unicorn to have a purple mane and tail, you should definitely run with that idea.

penguin

What other pet dresses in a formal tuxedo 24 hours a day? This pattern uses a small amount of white felt and a couple of different colors of yarn.

Head and Body:

Rnd 1: Starting at head with yarn A, make an adjustable ring, ch 1, work 6 sc into ring. Pull closed—6 sts. Insert a stitch marker into the loop on your hook. Each time you come back around to the stitch marker, move it up to the loop on your hook to begin the next round.

Rnd 2: *2 sc into next st, sc into next st; rep from * to end of rnd—9 sts.

Rnd 3: Sc into each st—9 sts.

Rnd 4: *2 sc into next st, sc into next 2 sts; rep from * to end of rnd—12 sts.

Rnds 5–12: Sc into each st.

Insert safety eyes between Rnds 3 and 4, 4 sts apart. Stuff firmly and continue.

Rnd 13: *2 sc into next st, sc into next 5 sts; rep from * to end of rnd—14 sts.

Rnd 14: *Invdec, sc into next 5 sts; rep from * to end of rnd—12 sts.

Rnd 15: Invdec around—6 sts.

- Fasten off with a slip stitch into the next sc, and leave a very long tail. Weave yarn tail through the last round of stitches, and pull tight to close the hole.

Wings (Make 2):

Row 1: With yarn A, ch 9. Dc into 4th ch from hook, dc in next ch, hdc in next 2 chs, sc in next ch, sl st in last ch—6 sts.

- Fasten off and leave a long tail for sewing. Sew the wing to the side of the body. Weave in ends.

- Repeat for the second wing.

Feet (Make 2):

Row 1: With yarn B, ch 6. 2 hdc into 3rd ch from hook, sl st in next ch, 2 hdc in next ch, sl st in last ch.

- Fasten off and sew foot to bottom front of body. Weave in ends.

- Repeat for second foot.

Beak:

Rnd 1: With yarn B, make an adjustable ring, ch 1, sc 3 into ring. Pull tail to close hole—3 sts.

- Fasten off and use yarn tail to sew beak to face of penguin.

Finishing:

- Cut a small teardrop from white felt. Snip off the small end. Stitch or glue into place with flat end on top.

Skill Level:
INTERMEDIATE

MATERIALS AND TOOLS

Black lightweight yarn (A) (refer to page 159 for a list of recommended yarns) **(3)**

Yellow lightweight yarn (B) **(3)**

Crochet hook: 2.75 mm (size C-2 U.S.)

Stitch marker

Yarn needle

Embroidery needle

Black embroidery floss

5-mm safety eyes, color of your choice

White felt

Polyester fiberfill stuffing

STITCHES AND TECHNIQUES USED

Adjustable ring, page 8

Chain (ch), page 6

Single crochet (sc), page 7

Invisible decrease (invdec), page 12

Slip stitch (sl st), page 7

Double crochet (dc), page 10

Half double crochet (hdc), page 9

Changing color, page 14

sloth

What is it about sloths that make them so endearing? They're slow and seem to always be smiling. The Sloth pattern here uses felt for the face and eye coloring. Use embroidery floss to stitch the nose if you have trouble finding an appropriately sized plastic one.

Head and Body:

- Before crocheting, cut a kidney shape from off-white felt and two tiny rectangles with rounded corners for the face. With sharp scissors, cut slits for inserting safety eyes in each rectangle shape and in the kidney-shaped piece. Cut a tiny slit in the center of the kidney-shaped piece for inserting the nose. Refer to photo. Set felt pieces aside. They can be trimmed to shape later if necessary.

Rnd 1: Starting at top of head, make an adjustable ring, ch 1, work 6 sc into ring. Pull closed—6 sts. Insert a stitch marker into the loop on your hook. Each time you come back around to the stitch marker, move it up to the loop on your hook to begin the next round.

Rnd 2: 2 sc into each st around—12 sts.

Rnd 3: *2 sc into next st, sc into each st around; rep from * to end of rnd—18 sts.

Rnds 4–6: Sc into each st—18 sts.

Rnd 7: *Invdec, sc into next 4 sts; rep from * to end of rnd—15 sts.

Rnd 8: *2 sc into next st, sc into next 2 sts; rep from * to end of rnd—20 sts.

Rnds 9–12: Sc into each st.

Rnd 13: *Invdec, sc into next 8 sts; rep from * to end of rnd—18 sts.

- Insert safety eyes into rectangles and kidney felt pieces, then into head between Rnds 3 and 4, 3 sts apart. Stuff head and body firmly and continue.

Rnd 14: *Invdec, sc into next st; rep from * to end of rnd—12 sts.

Skill Level:
INTERMEDIATE

MATERIALS AND TOOLS

Light brown lightweight yarn (refer to page 159 for a list of recommended yarns) (3)

Crochet hook: 2.75 mm (size C-2 U.S.)

Stitch marker

Yarn needle

Embroidery needle

Black embroidery floss

Brown felt

Off-white felt

5-mm safety eyes, color of your choice

5-mm safety animal nose

Scraps of gray yarn

Polyester fiberfill stuffing

STITCHES AND TECHNIQUES USED

Adjustable ring, page 8

Chain (ch), page 6

Single crochet (sc), page 7

Invisible decrease (invdec), page 12

Slip stitch (sl st), page 7

Half double crochet (hdc), page 9

Rnd 15: Invdec around—6 sts.

- Fasten off with a slip stitch into the next sc. Weave yarn tail through the last round of stitches, and pull tight to close the hole. Stitch or glue felt pieces down.

Arms (Make 2):

Rnd 1: Make an adjustable ring, ch 1, work 6 sc into ring. Pull closed—6 sts.

Rnd 2: *2 sc into next st, sc into next st; rep from * to end of rnd—9 sts.

Rnds 3–6: Sc into each st.

Rnd 7: Invdec, sc into each st—8 sts.

Rnds 8–11: Sc into each st.

Rnd 12: Invdec, sc into each st—7 sts.

- Fasten off and leave a long tail for sewing. Insert a little stuffing into arm. Sew to side of body. Weave in ends

- Repeat for second arm.

Feet (Make 2):

Row 1: Ch 5. Hdc into 3rd ch and next 2 chs—3 sts.

- Fasten off and sew foot to the bottom of the body. Weave in ends.

- Repeat for second foot.

Finishing:

- With black embroidery floss and an embroidery needle, stitch a small smile.

fox

Foxes have grown in popularity so much— wouldn't you love to have one for a pet? This one has black legs and an off-white tummy, achieved with simple color changes. A pet slicker brush used on each piece will make a fuzzy Fox.

Off-white lightweight yarn (A)
(refer to page 159 for a list of
recommended yarns) **③**

Dark orange lightweight yarn
(B) **③**

Black lightweight yarn (C) **③**

Crochet hook: 2.75 mm
(size C-2 U.S.)

Stitch marker

Yarn needle

Black embroidery floss

Embroidery needle

5-mm safety eyes (black or
colored)

7-mm safety animal nose

Polyester fiberfill stuffing

Chain (ch), page 6

Single crochet (sc), page 7

Half double crochet (hdc),
page 9

Double crochet (dc), page 10

Adjustable ring, page 8

Invisible decrease (invdec),
page 12

Slip stitch (sl st), page 7

Changing color, page 14

Chin Piece:

- The chin piece is crocheted
first and will be fitted over
the front lower section of
the head.

Row 1: Starting with yarn A,
ch 7, sc in 2nd ch from hook
and next st, hdc in next
2 chs, dc in next 2 chs—
6 sts.

Row 2: Ch 3, turn, dc in
2 sts, hdc in 2 sts, sc in 2
sts—6 sts.

Row 3: Ch 1, turn, sc in
2 sts, hdc in 2 sts, dc in 2
sts—6 sts.

- Fasten off and leave a long
tail for sewing. Set aside.

Head:

Rnd 1: Starting at nose end
of head, with yarn B, make
an adjustable ring, ch 1,
work 3 sc into ring. Pull
closed—3 sts. Insert a stitch
marker into the loop on your
hook. Each time you come
back around to the stitch
marker, move it up to the
loop on your hook to begin
the next round.

Rnd 2: 2 sc into next st, sc
into next st, 2 sc into next
st—5 sts.

Rnd 3: 2 sc into next st, sc
into each st around—6 sts.

Rnd 4: *2 sc into next st, sc
into next 2 sts; rep from * to
end of rnd—8 sts.

Rnd 5: 2 sc into each st—
16 sts.

Rnds 6–9: Sc into each st.

Rnd 10: Sc in next 2 sts,
invdec twice, sc in next 4 sts,
invdec twice, sc in next
2 sts—12 sts.

- Insert a stitch marker to
mark your place. Insert
safety eyes between Rnds 4
and 5, 4 sts apart. Stuff head.
Sew on chin piece.

Rnd 11: Invdec around—6 sts.

- Fasten off with a slip stitch
into the next sc. Weave yarn
tail through the last round
of stitches, and pull tight to
close the hole.

Body:

Rnd 1: With yarn B, make
an adjustable ring, ch 1, sc 6
into ring—6 sts. Pull ring to
close hole.

Rnd 2: 2 sc into each st—12 sts.

Rnds 3–9: Sc into next 4 sts,
change to yarn A, sc into
next 4 sts, change to yarn B,
sc into next 4 sts.—12 sts.

After Rnd 9, stuff body
firmly.

Rnd 10: Invdec around—6 sts.

- Fasten off and use a yarn needle and yarn tail to sew up last round of stitches.

- Sew head to top of front of body.

Legs (Make 4):

Rnd 1: With yarn C (black), make an adjustable ring, ch 1, sc 5 into ring. Pull tail to close hole—5 sts.

Rnds 2–6: Sc into each st.

Change to yarn B (orange) at end of Rnd 6.

Rnd 7: 2 sc into next st, sc into each st around—6 sts.

Rnd 8: Sc into each st.

- Fasten off and leave a long tail for sewing. Stuff leg sparingly, and sew leg to underside of body.

- Repeat for remaining three legs.

Ears (Make 2):

Rnd 1: With yarn C (black) make an adjustable ring, ch 1, sc 3 into ring. Pull tail to close hole—3 sts.

Rnd 2: 2 sc into each st—6 sts.

Change to yarn B (orange) at the end of Rnd 2.

Rnd 3: *2 sc into next st, sc into next st; rep from * to end of rnd—9 sts.

- Fasten off and leave a long tail. Flatten ear and sew to top of head. Weave in ends.

- Repeat for second ear.

Tail:

Rnd 1: With yarn A, make an adjustable ring, ch 1, sc 4 into ring. Pull tail to close hole—4 sts.

Rnd 2: *2 sc into next st, sc into next st; rep from * to end of rnd—6 sts.

Rnd 3: Sc into each st.

- Change to yarn B at end of Rnd 4.

Rnd 4: *2 sc into next st, sc into next 2 sts; rep from * to end of rnd—8 sts.

Rnds 5–7: Sc into each st.

Rnd 8: *Invdec, sc into 2 next sts; rep from * to end of rnd—6 sts.

Rnd 9: Sc into each st.

- Insert stitch marker to hold your place. Stuff tail sparingly.

Rnd 10: Invdec around—3 sts.

- Fasten off and sew tail to body.

Finishing:

- With black embroidery floss and an embroidery needle, stitch a mouth.

bear

If you met a bear cub in the wild, I'm sure you wouldn't be trying to leash it and bring it home, but as a Fantasy Pet, a bear cub would be an adorable addition to your home! This bear stands on all fours. Form the feet by stuffing the legs sparingly and bending the legs into shape. For a different color bear, change your yarn color. Brush the yarn with a slicker brush before assembling the pieces if you'd like a furry bear.

Head:

Rnd 1: Starting at nose, make an adjustable ring, ch 1, work 5 sc into ring. Pull closed—5 sts. Insert a stitch marker into the loop on your hook. Each time you come back around to the stitch marker, move it up to the loop on your hook to begin the next round.

Rnd 2: 2 sc into next st, sc into each st around—6 sts.

Rnd 3: Sc into each st.

Rnd 4: 2 sc into each st—12 sts.

Rnd 5: *2 sc into next st, sc into next st; rep from * to end of rnd—18 sts.

Rnds 6–8: Sc into each st.

Rnd 9: Invdec around—9 sts.

- Insert a stitch marker. Insert safety eyes between Rnds 3 and 4, 4 sts apart, and insert nose betweens Rnds 1 and 2. Stuff head firmly.

Rnd 10: *Invdec, sc into next st; rep from * to end of rnd—6 sts.

- Fasten off with a slip stitch into the next sc. Weave yarn tail through the last round of stitches, and pull tight to close the hole.

Body:

Rnd 1: Starting at front of body, which is the smaller end, make an adjustable ring, ch 1, sc 6 into ring. Pull tail to close hole—6 sts.

Rnd 2: 2 sc into each st—12 sts.

Rnd 3: Sc into each st.

Rnd 4: *2 sc into next st, sc into next 3 sts; rep from * to end of rnd—15 sts.

Rnd 5: Sc into each st.

Rnd 6: *2 sc into next st, sc into next 4 sts; rep from * to end of rnd—18 sts.

Rnds 7–9: Sc into each st.

Rnd 10: *2 sc into next st, sc into next 5 sts; rep from * to end of rnd—21 sts.

Rnd 11: Sc into each st.

Rnd 12: *Invdec, sc into next 5 sts; rep from * to end of rnd—18 sts.

Rnd 13: *Invdec, sc into next st; rep from * to end of rnd—12 sts.

- Insert a stitch marker to hold your place, and stuff body firmly.

Rnd 14: Invdec around—6 sts.

- Fasten off and close up hole by threading yarn tail through last round with a yarn needle. Weave in ends.

Skill Level:
INTERMEDIATE

MATERIALS AND TOOLS

Brown lightweight yarn (refer to page 159 for a list of recommended yarns) (3)

Crochet hook: 2.75 mm (size C-2 U.S.)

Stitch marker

Yarn needle

Black embroidery floss

5-mm black safety eyes

7-mm black animal nose

Embroidery needle

Polyester fiberfill stuffing

STITCHES AND TECHNIQUES USED

Adjustable ring, page 8

Chain (ch), page 6

Single crochet (sc), page 7

Invisble decrease (invdec), page 12

Front Legs (Make 2):

Rnd 1: Make an adjustable ring, ch 1, sc 6 into ring. Pull tail to close hole—6 sts.

Rnds 2–3: Sc into each st.

Rnd 4: 2 sc into next st, sc into each st around—7 sts.

Rnds 5–6: Sc into each st.

Rnd 7: 2 sc into next st, sc into each st around—8 sts.

Rnds 8–9: Sc into each st.

- Fasten off and leave a long tail for sewing. Stuff leg sparingly, and sew to front underside of body. Fold Rnds 1–3 to form foot. Stitch fold into place if desired.

- Repeat for second front leg.

Rear Legs (Make 2):

Rnd 1: Make an adjustable ring, ch 1, sc 6 into ring. Pull tail to close hole—6 sts.

Rnds 2–3: Sc into each st.

Rnd 4: 2 sc into next st, sc into each st around—7 sts.

Rnd 5: 2 sc into next st, sc into each st around—8 sts.

Rnd 6: Sc into each st.

Rnd 7: 2 sc into next st, sc into each st around—9 sts.

Rnds 8–9: Sc into each st.

Rnd 10: 2 sc into next st, sc into each st around—10 sts.

Rnd 11: Sc into each st.

- Fasten off and leave a long tail for sewing. Stuff leg sparingly, and sew to rear underside of body. Fold Rnds 1–3 to form foot. Stitch fold into place if desired.

- Repeat for second rear leg.

Ears (Make 2):

Rnd 1: Make an adjustable ring, ch 1, sc 5 into ring. Pull yarn tail to close ring. Fasten off.

- Stitch ear to top of head. Weave in ends.

- Repeat for second ear.

Finishing:

- With black embroidery floss and an embroidery needle, stitch a vertical line down from nose and small smile.

monkey

I think the attraction to any primate as a pet is how human-like they are! They have expressive faces and hug onto humans when held. Brush the pieces with a slicker brush for furry monkey hair.

Skill Level:
INTERMEDIATE

MATERIALS AND TOOLS

Black lightweight yarn (A) (refer to page 159 for a list of recommended yarns) (3)

Tan lightweight yarn (or color of your choice) (B) (3)

Crochet hook: 2.75 mm (size C-2 U.S.)

Stitch marker

Yarn needle

Embroidery needle

Black embroidery floss

5-mm black safety eyes (or color of your choice)

Polyester fiberfill stuffing

STITCHES AND TECHNIQUES USED

Adjustable ring, page 8

Chain (ch), page 6

Single crochet (sc), page 7

Invisible decrease (invdec), page 12

Bobble stitch, page 11

Slip stitch (sl st), page 7

Half double crochet (hdc), page 9

Changing color, page 14

Head:

Rnd 1: Starting at top of head with yarn A and C hook, make an adjustable ring, ch 1, work 6 sc into ring. Pull closed—6 sts. Insert a stitch marker into the loop on your hook. Each time you come back around to the stitch marker, move it up to the loop on your hook to begin the next round.

Rnd 2: 2 sc into each st around—12 sts.

Rnd 3: *2 sc into next st, sc into next st; rep from * to end of rnd—18 sts.

Rnd 4: *2 sc into next st, sc into next 5 sts; rep from * to end of rnd—21 sts.

Rnds 5–7: Sc into each st.

Rnd 8: *Invdec, sc into next 5 sts; rep from * to end of rnd—18 sts.

Rnd 9: *Invdec, sc into next st; rep from * to end of rnd—12 sts.

- Insert stitch marker to hold your place, and stuff the head.

Rnd 10: Invdec around—6 sts.

- Fasten off and leave a long tail. Close up hole by weaving tail through last round. Weave in ends.

Body:

Rnd 1: With yarn A, make an adjustable ring, ch 1, and 6 sc into ring. Pull tail to close ring—6 sts.

Rnd 2: 2 sc into each st—12 sts.

Rnd 3: *2 sc into next st, sc into next st; rep from * to end of rnd—18 sts.

Rnds 4–9: Sc into each st.

Rnd 10: *Invdec, sc into next 4 sts; rep from * to end of rnd—15 sts.

- Fasten off and leave a long tail. Stuff body. Sew to head with yarn tail. Weave in ends.

Arms (Make 2):

Rnd 1: With black yarn A, make an adjustable ring, ch 1, sc 6 into ring. Pull tail to close ring—6 sts.

Rnds 2–11: Sc into each st.

- Change to tan yarn B at end of Rnd 11.

Rnd 12: Sc into each st.

Rnd 13: 2 sc into next st, sc into each st around—7 sts.

- Insert a stitch marker to hold your place and stuff arm.

Rnd 14: Make a bobble [4 dc] into next st, sc into each st around—7 sts.

Rnd 15: Invdec, sc into each st—6 sts.

- Fasten off and use yarn tail to close up hole by weaving through last round of stitches with a yarn needle. Weave in ends. Sew each arm to side of body.

- Repeat for second arm.

Legs (Make 2):

Rnd 1: With black yarn A, make an adjustable ring, ch 1, sc 6 into ring. Pull tail to close ring—6 sts.

Rnd 2: Sc into each st.

Rnd 3: 2 sc into next st, sc into each st—7 sts.

Rnd 4: Sc into each st.

Rnds 5–6: Sl st into next 3 sts, hdc into next 4 sts—7 sts.

Rnds 7–8: Sc into each st.

Rnd 9: 2 sc into next st, sc into each st—8 sts.

Rnd 10: Sc into each st.

- Fasten off and stuff leg sparingly. Set aside.

- Repeat for second leg.

Feet (Make 2):

Row 1: With tan yarn B, ch 11, sc into 2nd ch and next 9 chs—10 sts.

Rows 2–3: Ch 1, turn, sc into each st.

- Fasten off and leave a long tail for sewing. Fold in half, and sew edges closed with yarn tail. Sew to open end of leg.

- Repeat for second foot.

- Sew each assembled leg to bottom of body. Stitch legs into a bent position if desired.

Face:

Row 1: Starting at bottom of face with tan yarn B, ch 6. Sc into 2nd ch from hook and next 4 chs—5 sts.

Row 2: Ch 1, turn, sc into 2 sts, 2 sc into next st, sc into 2 sts—6 sts.

Row 3: Ch 1, turn, sc into each st.

Row 4: Ch 1, turn, invdec, sc into next 2 sts, invdec—4 sts.

Row 5: Ch 1, turn, (sc, hdc) into first st, sc in next 2 sts, (hdc, sc) in last st—6 sts.

- Fasten off and leave a long tail for sewing.

- Insert safety eyes into face between Rows 4 and 5, 2 sts apart.

- Sew face to head. Weave in ends.

Mouth:

Rnd 1: With yarn B make an adjustable ring, ch 1, sc 6 into ring. Pull tail to close hole—6 sts.

Rnd 2: *2 sc into next st, sc into next st; rep from * to end of rnd—9 sts.

Rnds 3-4: Sc into each st.

- Fasten off and leave a long tail. Sew to face, stuffing a little as you sew the last stitches closed.

Finishing:

- With black embroidery floss and embroidery needle, stitch tiny straight horizontal stitches for nostrils.

- With black embroidery floss, stitch a wide smile across the mouth.

pony/
unicorn

All little girls wish for a pony at least once, don't they? I did. If not a pony, how about a unicorn? This is the Fantasy Pets chapter, after all. This small-scaled horse will never grow up, and you don't have to either. Add a golden horn and magical colors to get a unicorn, as detailed below. I used white yarn with iridescence for the unicorn to give it an extra sparkle.

Head:

Rnd 1: Starting at nose end of head with yarn A, make an adjustable ring, ch 1, work 6 sc into ring. Pull closed—6 sts. Insert a stitch marker into the loop on your hook. Each time you come back around to the stitch marker, move it up to the loop on your hook to begin the next round.

Rnd 2: 2 sc into each st—12 sts.

Rnd 3: *2 sc into next st, sc into next 3 sts; rep from * to end of rnd—15 sts.

Rnds 4–8: Sc into each st around.

Rnd 9: *2 sc into next st, sc into next 4 sts; rep from * to end of rnd—18 sts.

Rnds 10–13: Sc into each st.

Rnd 14: *Invdec, sc into next st; rep from * to end of rnd—12 sts.

- Insert stitch marker to hold your place. Insert eyes between Rnds 6 and 7, 4 sts apart. Stuff head.

Rnd 15: Invdec around—6 sts.

- Fasten off and leave a long tail. Weave tail through the last round of stitches in Rnd 15 to close the hole. Weave in ends. Set aside.

Body:

Rnd 1: Starting at front of body with yarn A, make an adjustable ring, ch 1, sc 6 into ring. Pull tail to close ring—6 sts.

Rnd 2: 2 sc into each st—12 sts.

Rnd 3: *2 sc into next st, sc into next st; rep from * to end of rnd—18 sts.

Rnd 4: *2 sc into next st, sc into next 2 sts; rep from * to end of rnd—24 sts.

Rnd 5: *2 sc into next st, sc into next 7 sts; rep from * to end of rnd—27 sts.

Rnds 6–15: Sc into each st.

Rnd 16: *2 sc into next st, sc into next 8 sts; rep from * to end of rnd—30 sts.

Rnds 17–19: Sc into each st.

Rnd 20: *Invdec, sc into next 3 sts; rep from * to end of rnd—24 sts.

Rnd 21: Invdec around—12 sts.

Insert a stitch marker, and stuff body.

Rnd 22: Invdec around—6 sts.

- Fasten off and use yarn needle to weave tail through last round to close hole.

Skill Level:
INTERMEDIATE

MATERIALS AND TOOLS

Lightweight yarn (main color of your choice) (A) (refer to page 159 for a list of recommended yarns) (3)

Lightweight yarn (tail and mane color of your choice) (B) (3)

Gray lightweight yarn (C) (3)

Gold lightweight yarn (unicorn only) (D) (3)

Crochet hook: 2.75 mm (size C-2 U.S.)

Stitch marker

Yarn needle

Embroidery needle

5-mm safety eyes

Black embroidery floss

Polyester fiberfill stuffing

(continued on page 136)

Neck:

Rnd 1: With yarn A, ch 14. Join with a sl st to first ch to form a ring. Sc in each ch—14 sts.

Rnds 2–5: Sc into each st.

- Fasten off and leave a long tail. Sew neck to top of body, and insert a little stuffing. Sew head to neck at an angle. Weave in ends.

Front Legs (Make 2):

Rnd 1: With yarn C, make an adjustable ring, ch 1, sc 8 into ring. Pull tail to close ring—8 sts.

Rnd 2: Working into back loops only (BLO), sc into each st—8 sts.

- Change to yarn A at the end of Rnd 2.

Rnds 3–4: Sc into each st.

Rnd 5: Invdec, sc into each st—7 sts.

Rnds 6–8: Sc into each st.

Rnd 9: 2 sc into next st, sc into each st around—8 sts.

Rnd 10: Sc into each st.

Rnd 11: Invdec, sc into each st—7 sts.

Rnd 12: Sc into each st.

Rnd 13: 2 sc into next 2 sts, sc into next 5 sts—9 sts.

Rnd 14: Sc into each st.

Rnd 15: 2 sc into next st, sc into each st—10 sts.

Rnds 16–18: Sc into each st.

- Fasten off and leave a long tail. Stuff leg and flatten top; sew to side of ody.

- Repeat for second front leg.

Rear legs (Make 2):

Rnd 1: With yarn C, make an adjustable ring, ch 1, sc 8 into ring. Pull tail to close ring—8 sts.

Rnd 2: Working into back loops only (BLO), sc into each st—8 sts.

- Change to yarn A at the end of Rnd 2.

Rnds 3–4: Sc into each st.

Rnd 5: Invdec, sc into each st—7 sts.

Rnds 6–8: Sc into each st.

Rnd 9: 2 sc into next st, sc into each st around—8 sts.

Rnd 10: Sc into each st.

Rnd 11: Invdec, sc into each st—7 sts.

Rnd 12: Sc into each st.

Rnd 13: 2 sc into next 2 sts, sc into next 5 sts—9 sts.

Rnd 14: 2 sc into next st, sc into each st—10 sts.

Rnd 15: *2 sc into next st, sc into next 4 sts; rep from * to end of rnd—12 sts.

Rnds 16–19: Sc into each st.

- Fasten off and leave a long tail. Stuff leg and flatten top; sew to side of body.

- Repeat for second rear leg.

Ears (Make 2):

Row 1: With yarn A, ch 6. Hdc into 3rd ch from hook, hdc into next ch, sc in next ch, sl st into last ch—4 sts.

- Fasten off and sew ear to the side of the head.

- Repeat for second ear.

Mane:

Row 1: With yarn B, ch 12. Sew ch to head and down neck to body.

- Cut 24 pieces of yarn 3 inches (7.6 cm) long. Hook 2 strands into each ch for mane. Trim as desired.

Horn (unicorn only):

Rnd 1: With yarn D, make an adjustable ring, ch 1, sc 3 into ring. Pull tail to close ring—3 sts.

Rnd 2: 2 sc into next st, sc into each st—4 sts.

Rnds 3–4: Sc into each st.

Rnd 5: 2 sc into next st, sc into each st—5 sts.

Rnds 6–8: Sc into each st.

Rnd 9: 2 sc into next st, sc into each st—6 sts.

- Fasten off and stitch to top of head between ears. Weave in ends.

Finishing:

- With black embroidery floss, stitch nostrils with tiny straight stitches on nose.

- With black embroidery floss, stitch mouth with one long straight stitch.

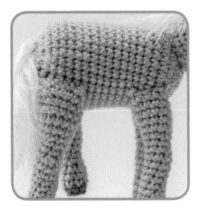

dragon

Why a pet dragon? Why NOT a pet dragon? This one has horns, wings, spikes on his back, and a long curving tail! Change the colors of anything for a totally different look.

Head:

Rnd 1: With yarn A, make an adjustable ring, ch 1, sc 6 into ring—6 sts.

Rnd 2: 2 sc into each st around—12 sts.

Rnd 3: *2 sc into next st, sc into next st; rep from * to end of rnd—18 sts.

Rnd 4: *2 sc into next st, sc into next 2 sts; rep from * to end of rnd—24 sts.

Rnds 5–10: Sc into each st.

Rnd 11: *2 sc into next st, sc into next 7 sts; rep from * to end of rnd—27 sts.

Rnd 12: Sc into each st.

Rnd 13: *2 sc into next st, sc into next 8 sts; rep from * to end of rnd—30 sts.

Rnds 14–18: Sc into each st.

Rnd 19: *Invdec, sc into next 3 sts; rep from * to end of rnd—24 sts.

Rnd 20: Invdec around—12 sts.

- Insert a stitch marker to hold your place. Insert safety eyes into head between Rnds 11 and 12, 6 sts apart. Stuff head firmly.

Rnd 21: Invdec around—6 sts.

- Fasten off and leave a long tail. Sew hole closed with yarn tail and yarn needle.

Body:

Rnd 1: Starting at the front of the body with yarn A, make an adjustable ring, ch 1, sc 6 into ring. Pull tail to close hole—6 sts.

Rnd 2: 2 sc into each st— 12 sts.

Rnd 3: *2 sc into next st, sc into next st; rep from * to end of rnd—18 sts.

Rnd 4: *2 sc into next st, sc into next 2 sts; rep from * to end of rnd—24 sts.

Rnd 5: *2 sc into next st, sc into next 3 sts; rep from * to end of rnd—30 sts.

Rnd 6: *2 sc into next st, sc into next 4 sts; rep from * to end of rnd—36 sts.

Rnd 7: *2 sc into next st, sc into next 5 sts; rep from * to end of rnd—42 sts.

Rnds 8–13: Sc into each st.

Rnd 14: *Invdec, sc into next 12 sts; rep from * to end of rnd—39 sts.

Rnds 15-19: Sc into each st.

Rnd 20: *Invdec, sc into next 11 sts; rep from * to end of rnd—36 sts.

Rnds 21-30: Sc into each st.

Rnd 31: *2 sc into next st, sc into next 11 sts; rep from * to end of rnd—39 sts.

Skill Level:
INTERMEDIATE

MATERIALS AND TOOLS

Green lightweight yarn (A) (refer to page 159 for a list of recommended yarns) **3**

Yellow lightweight yarn (B) **3**

Purple lightweight yarn (C) **3**

Crochet hook: 2.75 mm (size C-2 U.S.)

Stitch marker

9-mm safety eyes

Yarn needle

Embroidery needle

Black embroidery floss

Polyester fiberfill stuffing

(continued on page 140)

Rnds 32–36: Sc into each st.

Rnd 37: *Invdec, sc into next 11 sts; rep from * to end of rnd—36 sts.

Rnd 38: Invdec 6 times, sc into next 24 sts—30 sts.

Rnd 39: Invdec 3 times, sc into next 24 sts—27 sts.

Rnd 40: *Invdec, sc into next 7 sts; rep from * to end of rnd—24 sts.

Rnd 41: *Invdec, sc into next 6 sts; rep from * to end of rnd—21 sts.

Rnd 42: Sc into each st.

Rnds 43–47: Sc into 7 sts, hdc into 7 sts, sc into 7 sts—21 sts.

Rnd 48: Invdec, sc into 5 sts, hdc into 7 sts, sc into 7 sts—20 sts.

Rnd 49: Sc into 6 sts, hdc into 7 sts, invdec, sc into 5 sts—19 sts.

Rnd 50: Invdec, sc into each st—18 sts.

Rnd 51: Sc into each st.

- Insert a stitch marker to hold your place and stuff body.

Rnds 52–54: Hdc into first 4 sts, sc in next 12 sts, hdc in next 2 sts—18 sts.

Rnd 55: Hdc into first 4 sts, invdec, sc in next 8 sts, invdec, hdc in next 2 sts—16 sts.

Rnd 56: Hdc into first 4 sts, sc in next 10 sts, hdc in next 2 sts—16 sts.

Rnd 57: Hdc into first 4 sts, sc in next 4 sts, invdec, sc in next 4 sts, hdc in next 2 sts—15 sts.

Rnd 58: Hdc into first 4 sts, sc in next 9 sts, hdc in next 2 sts—15 sts.

Rnd 59: Hdc into first 4 sts, sc in next 3 sts, invdec, sc in next 4 sts, hdc in next 2 sts—14 sts.

Rnd 60: Invdec, sc in each st around—13 sts.

Rnd 61: Invdec, sc in each st around—12 sts.

Rnd 62: Invdec, sc in each st around—11 sts.

Rnd 63: Invdec, sc in each st around—10 sts.

Rnd 64: Sc into each st.

- Insert a stitch marker to hold your place, and stuff the rest of the body and the tail.

Rnd 65: Invdec, sc in each st around—9 sts.

Rnd 66: *Invdec, sc in next st; rep from * to end of rnd—6 sts.

- Fasten off and weave yarn tail through last round to close hole. Weave in ends.

Neck:

Rnd 1: With yarn A, ch 21. Join to first ch with a sl st to form a ring. Sc in each ch—21 sts.

Rnds 2–4: Sc in each st.

Rnd 5: Invdec, sc in each st—20 sts.

Rnd 6: Sc in each st.

Rnd 7: Invdec, sc in each st—19 sts.

Rnd 8: Sc in each st.

Rnd 9: Invdec, sc in each st—18 sts.

Rnd 10: Sc in each st.

- Fasten off and leave a long tail for sewing.

- Stitch into place on the top front of the body. Stuff neck firmly. Sew head to top of neck. Weave in ends.

Legs (Make 4):

Rnd 1: With yarn A, make an adjustable ring, ch 1, sc 6 into ring. Pull tail to close ring—6 sts.

Rnd 2: 2 sc in next st—12 sts.

Rnd 3: *2 sc in next st, sc in next st; rep from * to end of rnd—18 sts.

Rnds 4–6: Sc in each st.

Rnd 7: Invdec, sc in each st—17 sts.

Rnds 8–11: Sc in each st.

Rnd 12: Invdec, sc in each st—16 sts.

Rnds 13–14: Sc in each st.

Rnd 15: Invdec, sc in each st—15 sts.

Rnds 16–17: Sc in each st.

Rnd 18: 2 Hdc in first 5 sts, sc in next 10 sts—20 sts.

Rnd 19: *2 hdc in next st, hdc in next st; rep from * 4 more times, sc in next 10—25 sts.

Rnd 20: Sc in each st.

- Fasten off and stuff. Set aside.

- Repeat 3 times for remaining legs.

Sole of Foot (Make 4):

Rnd 1: With yarn A, ch 4. Sc in 2nd ch from hook and next ch, hdc 8 in last ch, working around to the other side of ch, sc in next 2 chs, 3 sc in last ch—15 sts.

Rnd 2: Sc in next 4 sts, 2 hdc in next 2 sts, hdc in next 2 sts, 2 hdc in next 2 sts, sc in next 5 sts—19 sts.

Rnd 3: Sc in next 5 sts, 2 hdc in next st, hdc in next 2 sts, 2 hdc in next 2 sts, hdc in next 2 sts, 2 hdc in next st, sc in next 6 sts—23 sts.

- Fasten off and leave a long tail. Repeat for remaining three soles. Sew each sole to the bottom of a leg. Weave in ends.

Horns (Make 4):

Rnd 1: With yarn B make an adjustable ring, ch 1, sc 3 into ring. Pull tail to close hole—3 sts.

Rnd 2: 2 sc in first st, sc in each st—4 sts.

Rnd 3: 2 sc in first st, sc in each st—5 sts.

Rnds 4–5: Sc in each st.

- Fasten off and leave a long tail. Sew each horn to the top of the head, two further forward and spread farther apart, and two further back on the head and closer together. Weave in ends.

Back and Tail Spikes (Make 6):

Rnd 1: With yarn B make an adjustable ring, ch 1, sc 3 into ring. Pull tail to close hole—3 sts.

Rnd 2: 2 sc in each st—6 sts.

Rnd 3: *2 sc in next st, sc in next st; rep from * to end of rnd—9 sts.

Rnd 4: 2 sc in next st, sc in each st around—10 sts.

- Fasten off and leave a long tail for sewing. Repeat 5 times. Flatten spike and sew along neck, back, and tail evenly spaced apart. Weave in ends.

Wings (Make 2):

Row 1: With yarn C, ch 11. Sc into 2nd ch from hook and next 9 sts—10 sts.

Row 2: Ch 1, turn, 2 sc in first st, sc in next 7 sts, invdec—10 sts.

Row 3: Ch 1, turn, invdec, sc in next 7 sts, 2 sc in last st—10 sts.

Row 4: Ch 1, turn, sc in each st.

Row 5: Ch 1, turn, invdec, sc in next 7 sts, 2 sc in last st—10 sts.

Row 6: Ch 1, turn, invdec, sc in next 6 sts, invdec—8 sts.

Row 7: Ch 1, turn, invdec, sc in next 4 sts, invdec—6 sts.

Row 8: Ch 1, turn, sc in each st.

Row 9: Ch 1, turn, invdec, sc in next 2 sts, invdec—4 sts.

Row 10: Ch 1, turn, sc in each st.

Row 11: Ch 1, turn, invdec twice—2 sts.

Row 12: Ch 1, turn, invdec—1 st.

Row 13: Ch 1, turn to work edge, sc 6 evenly, 2 sc in corner, sc 5 evenly, 2 sc in corner, turning to work bottom edge, sc in first st, hdc in next st, dc in next st, trc in next st, dc in next st, hdc in next st, sc in next 2 sts, turning to work up side, 2 sc in corner, sc 12 evenly along edge, 3 sc in last st—40 sts.

- Fasten off and leave a long tail for sewing. Stitch wing to back with curving edge created along the bottom in Row 13 toward the rear of the dragon.

- Repeat for second wing.

Finishing:

- With black embroidery floss and embroidery needle, stitch wide smile on the front of the head.

- Stitch two nostrils on the front of the head.

- Thread a yarn needle with yellow yarn B, and stitch three "claws" on the front of each foot. Weave in ends.

dinosaur

Thank goodness we don't even have the option to have a pet dinosaur! If you did, I'll bet you'd take home this little T-rex, wouldn't you? Change the colors for a different look. I added stripes all along the back with a marker, which keeps the scaly look that comes naturally from the crochet stitches, and makes your dinosaur totally customizable! If you want a meaner dino, make a more menacing mouth and eyes.

MATERIALS AND TOOLS

Tan lightweight yarn
(refer to page 159 for a list
of recommended yarns) **3**

Crochet hook: 2.75 mm
(size C-2 U.S.)

Stitch marker

9-mm cat/reptile safety eyes

Yarn needle

Embroidery needle

Black embroidery floss

Polyester fiberfill stuffing

Permanent markers (black,
brown, blue, and/or green)

STITCHES AND TECHNIQUES USED

Adjustable ring, page 8

Chain (ch), page 6

Single crochet (sc), page 7

Invisible decrease (invdec),
page 12

Half double crochet (hdc),
page 9

Slip stitch (sl st), page 7

Double crochet (dc), page 10

Head:

Rnd 1: Make an adjustable
ring, ch 1, sc 6 into ring—
6 sts.

Rnd 2: 2 sc into each st
around—12 sts.

Rnd 3: *2 sc into next st, sc
into next st; rep from * to
end of rnd—18 sts.

Rnd 4: *2 sc into next st, sc
into next 2 sts; rep from * to
end of rnd—24 sts.

Rnds 5–10: Sc into each st.

Rnd 11: *2 sc into next st, sc
into next 7 sts; rep from * to
end of rnd—27 sts.

Rnds 12–13: Sc into each st.

Rnd 14: *2 sc into next st, sc
into next 8 sts; rep from * to
end of rnd—30 sts.

Rnds 15–19: Sc into each st.

Rnd 20: *Invdec, sc into next
3 sts; rep from * to end of
rnd—24 sts.

Rnd 21: *Invdec, sc into next
2 sts; rep from * to end of
rnd—18 sts.

- Insert a stitch marker to
hold your place. Insert safety
eyes into head between Rnds
12 and 13, 11 sts apart. Stuff
head firmly.

Rnd 22: *Invdec, sc into
next st; rep from * to end of
rnd—12 sts.

Rnd 23: Invdec around—6 sts.

- Fasten off and leave a long
tail. Sew hole closed with
yarn tail and yarn needle.

Tail and Body:

Rnd 1: Starting at the tip of
the tail, make an adjustable
ring, ch 1, sc 5 into ring. Pull
tail to close hole—5 sts.

Rnds 2–3: Sc into each st.

Rnd 4: 2 sc into next st, sc
into each st around—6 sts.

Rnd 5: 2 sc into next st, sc
into each st around—7 sts.

Rnds 6–7: Sc into each st.

Rnd 8: 2 sc into next st, sc
into each st around—8 sts.

Rnd 9: 2 sc into next st, sc
into each st around—9 sts.

Rnd 10: 2 sc into next st, sc
into each st around—10 sts.

Rnd 11: *2 sc into next st, sc
into next 4 sts; rep from * to
end of rnd—12 sts.

Rnd 12: *2 sc into next st, sc
into next 5 sts; rep from * to
end of rnd—14 sts.

Rnd 13: Sc into each st.

Rnd 14: 2 sc into next st, sc
into each st around—15 sts.

Rnd 15: Sc into each st.

Rnd 16: 2 sc into next st, sc
into each st around—16 sts.

Rnd 17: *2 sc into next st, sc into next 7 sts; rep from * to end of rnd—18 sts.

Rnd 18: *2 sc into next st, sc into next 5 sts; rep from * to end of rnd—21 sts.

Rnd 19: Sc into each st.

Rnd 20: *2 sc into next st, sc into next 6 sts; rep from * to end of rnd—24 sts.

Rnds 21–22: Sc into each st.

Rnd 23: *2 sc into next st, sc into next 7 sts; rep from * to end of rnd—27 sts.

Rnd 24: Sc into each st.

Rnd 25: *2 sc into next st, sc into next 8 sts; rep from * to end of rnd—30 sts.

Rnd 26: *2 sc into next st, sc into next 9 sts; rep from * to end of rnd—33 sts.

Rnd 27: *2 sc into next st, sc into next 10 sts; rep from * to end of rnd—36 sts.

Rnds 28–29: Sc into each st.

Rnd 30: *2 sc into next st, sc into next 11 sts; rep from * to end of rnd—39 sts.

Rnd 31: Sc into each st.

Rnd 32: *2 sc into next st, sc into next 12 sts; rep from * to end of rnd—42 sts.

Rnds 33–35: Hdc into 21 sts, sc into 21 sts—42 sts.

Rnd 36: Hdc into 21 sts, *invdec, sc into next 5 sts; rep from * to end of rnd—39 sts.

Rnds 37–38: Hdc into 21 sts, sc into 18 sts—39 sts.

Rnd 39: *Invdec, sc into next 11 sts; rep from * to end of rnd—36 sts.

Rnd 40: *Invdec, sc into next 5 sts; rep from * twice more, sc into next 15 sts—33 sts.

Rnd 41: *Invdec, sc into next 4 sts; rep from * twice more, sc into next 15 sts—30 sts.

Rnd 42: Sc into each st.

Rnd 43: *Invdec, sc into next 8 sts; rep from * to end of rnd—27 sts.

Rnd 44: Sc into each st.

Rnd 45: *Invdec, sc into next 7 sts; rep from * to end of rnd—24 sts.

Rnd 46: Sc into next 6 sts, hdc in next 12 sts, sc in next 6 sts—24 sts.

- Insert a stitch marker to mark your place, and stuff tail and body firmly.

Rnd 47: *Invdec, sc into next 2 sts; rep from * to end of rnd—18 sts.

Rnd 48: Sc in first 3 sts, hdc in next 9 sts, sc in next 6 sts—18 sts.

Rnds 49–55: Sc into each st.

Rnd 56: *Invdec, sc into next 7 sts; rep from * to end of rnd—16 sts.

Rnds 57–59: Sc into each st.

- Fasten off and leave a long yarn tail for sewing. Completely stuff neck, and sew on head. Weave in ends.

Legs (Make 2):

Rnd 1: Starting at top of leg, make an adjustable ring, ch 1, sc 6 into ring. Pull tail to close ring—6 sts.

Rnd 2: 2 sc in next st—12 sts.

Rnd 3: *2 sc in next st, sc in next st; rep from * to end of rnd—18 sts.

Rnd 4: *2 sc in next st, sc in next 2 sts; rep from * to end of rnd—24 sts.

Rnds 5–7: Sc in each st.

Rnd 8: Invdec, sc in each st—23 sts.

Rnd 9: Invdec, sc in each st—22 sts.

Rnd 10: Invdec, sc in each st—21 sts.

Rnd 11: *Invdec, sc in next 5 sts; rep from * to end of rnd—18 sts.

Rnd 12: Sc into each st.

Rnd 13: Invdec, sc in each st—17 sts.

Rnd 14: Invdec, sc in each st—16 sts.

Rnd 15: Invdec, sc in each st—15 sts.

Rnd 16: Sc in each st.

Rnds 17–19: Hdc in next 7 sts, sc in 8 sts—15 sts.

Rnd 20: Hdc in next 7 sts, sl st in 8 sts—15 sts.

Rnd 21: Invdec, sc in each st—14 sts.

Rnd 22: Invdec, sc in each st—13 sts.

Rnd 23: Invdec, sc in each st—12 sts.

Rnd 24: Invdec, sc in each st—11 sts.

Rnd 25: Invdec, sc in each st—10 sts.

Rnd 26: *2 sc in next st, sc in next 4 sts; rep from * to end of rnd—12 sts.

Rnd 27: *2 sc in next st, sc in next st; rep from * to end of rnd—18 sts.

Rnd 28: Sc in next 9 sts, *ch 5, sc in 2nd ch from hook and next ch, hdc in next ch, dc in last ch, skip next st in round, sl st in next st (toe made); rep from * twice more, sc into next 3 sts—12 sts and 3 toes.

Rnd 29: Sc in 12 sts, working around tip of toe, 2 sc in tip of toe, sc in next 8 sts, 2 sc in tip of toe, sc in next 8 sts, 2 sc in tip of toe, sc in next 8 sts—42 sts.

- Fasten off and leave a long tail for sewing. Stuff leg and set aside.

- Repeat for remaining leg.

Sole (Make 2):

Rnd 1: Make an adjustable ring, ch 1, sc 6 into ring. Pull tail to close ring—6 sts.

Rnd 2: 2 sc into each st—12 sts.

Rnd 3: *2 sc into next st, sc into next st; rep from * to end of rnd—18 sts.

Rnd 4: Making toes, *ch 5, sc into 2nd ch from hook and next ch, hdc into next ch, dc into next ch, skip next st in round, sl st into next st; rep from * twice more, sc in 12 sts—12 sts and 3 toes.

Rnd 5: Working around toes, sc in next 4, 2 sc in tip of toe, sc in 8 sts, 2 sc in tip of toe, sc in 8 sts, 2 sc in tip of toe, sc in 16 sts—42 sts

- Fasten off and leave a long tail for sewing. Repeat for second sole. Stitch each sole to the bottom of a leg, inserting stuffing as you close up last stitches. Weave in ends.

- Sew each leg to side of body.

Arms (Make 2):

Rnd 1: Make an adjustable ring, ch 1, sc 6 into ring. Pull tail to close ring—6 sts.

Rnds 2–8: Sc into each st.

- Insert a small amount of stuffing. Flatten arm. You will work into both layers of arm to close the end.

Row 9: Ch 1, sc through both layers across—3 sts.

Rnd 10: Ch 2, turn, (hdc, sl st) into first st, ch 2, (hdc, sl st) into second st, ch 2, (hdc, sl st) into last st—3 fingers made.

- Fasten off and weave in ends. Sew arm to side of body.

- Repeat for second arm.

Finishing:

- With black embroidery floss and embroidery needle, stitch wide menacing smile on the front of the head.

- Stitch two nostrils with black embroidery floss.

- Thread a yarn needle and stitch across the top of each eye several times for eyelids. Weave in ends.

- Use permanent markers to lightly mark stripes along the dino's neck, back, and tail in your desired pattern.

accessories

So you've made your favorite pet out of yarn. If you're finished, your new pet needs some supplies. Start with a place to sleep. Crochet either a big cushy rectangular bed or a fancy bolstered bed. Make a collar and leash, and don't forget a few toys to keep him busy. A food and water bowl with his name stitched on will be a necessity. You can even give your fish a tiny aquarium.

All of these items make playing with these AmiguruME Pets lots of fun, especially if they are a gift. Everything in this section is customizable. Change the bed colors easily. Substitute yarn colors for the toys, and the sky's the limit for a collar and tag.

Bone

Your crocheted AmiguruME dog will yelp for joy when you make this bone to accompany him. Even a pet T-rex would undoubtedly love this accessory. Crochet a toy bone in red or another bright color to resemble the rubber ones available at pet stores.

INSTRUCTIONS

Rnd 1: Make an adjustable ring, ch 1, sc 4 into ring. Pull tail to close ring—4 sts.

Rnd 2: *2 sc into next st, sc into next st; rep from * to end of rnd—6 sts.

Rnd 3: Sc into each st.

- Fasten off and cut tail short.

- Repeat Rnds 1–3. Do not fasten off.

Rnd 4: Sc into next 3 sts, hold first piece next to second and sc into st on first piece, joining the two rounded ends of the bone, sc into next sc, invdec, sc into next 2, join to second piece again with a sc, invdec—10 sts.

Rnd 5: Invdec, sc in next st, invdec twice, sc in next st, invdec—6 sts.

Rnds 6–11: Sc into each st.

- Fasten off and leave a long tail for sewing. Stuff firmly. Set aside.

- Repeat Rnds 1–5, creating another bone end with two bumps. Stuff and sew pieces together. Weave in ends.

MATERIALS AND TOOLS

White lightweight yarn (refer to page 159 for a list of recommended yarns) (3)

Crochet hook: 2.75mm (size C-2 U.S.)

Stitch marker

Yarn needle

Polyester fiberfill stuffing

STITCHES AND TECHNIQUES USED

Adjustable ring, page 8

Chain (ch), page 6

Single crochet (sc), page 7

Invisible decrease (invdec), page 12

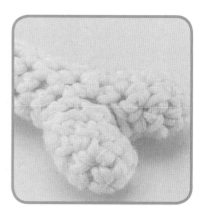

Rectangle Bed

If you have a big dog or a cat that likes to really stretch out, crochet a rectangle bed. Your pet sloth will probably enjoy it too. This bed is very easy to customize. I made a plaid pattern on the top surface, but you can use variegated yarn, stitch stripes, or even embroider flowers all over the bed for a different look. Instructions for making the bed smaller or larger are included below.

INSTRUCTIONS

Bed Panel (make one with YARN A and one with YARN B):

*Note: To make bed larger, increase the number of stitches in the beginning ch and the number of rows. For a smaller bed, decrease the number of beginning chs and number of rows.

Row 1: With yarn A, ch 35. Sc into 2nd ch from hook and next 33 chs—34 sts.

Rows 2–25: Ch 1, turn, sc into each st.

- Fasten off and leave a very long tail. Set aside.

- Repeat with yarn B.

MATERIALS AND TOOLS

Blue lightweight yarn (A) (refer to page 159 for a list of recommended yarns) (3)

Off-white lightweight yarn (B) (3)

Crochet hook: 2.75 mm (size C-2 U.S.)

Stitch marker

Yarn needle

Embroidery needle

Black and yellow embroidery floss

Polyester fiberfill stuffing

STITCHES AND TECHNIQUES USED

Chain (ch), page 6

Single crochet (sc), page 7

Plaid pattern:

- With black embroidery floss and embroidery needle, stitch straight lines vertically and horizontally, several rows apart, to form a checkerboard pattern.

- Repeat with yellow embroidery floss, offset between the black pattern, stitching lines vertically and horizontally.

Assembly:

- With blue yarn tail, seam edges all the way around, inserting stuffing as you close up the last few stitches. Weave in ends.

Bolster Bed

My dogs love to curl up in their beds with a bolster. Animals that like to snuggle will love this type of pet bed. For a simple oval bed, leave off the bolster.

Skill Level:
INTERMEDIATE

INSTRUCTIONS

Bottom Bed Panel:

Rnd 1: Ch 6, sc into 2nd ch from hook and next 3 chs, 5 sc in last ch, working around to other side of ch, sc in next 4 chs, 5 sc in last ch—18 sts. Insert a stitch marker into the loop on your hook. Each time you come back around to the stitch marker, move it up to the loop on your hook to begin the next round.

Rnd 2: Sc into next 5 sts, 2 sc into next 3 sts, sc into next 6 sts, 2 sc into next 3 sts, sc in last st—24 sts.

Rnd 3: *2 sc into next st, sc into next 3 sts; rep from * to end of rnd—30 sts.

Rnd 4: *2 sc into next st, sc into next 4 sts; rep from * to end of rnd—36 sts.

Rnd 5: *2 sc into next st, sc into next 5 sts; rep from * to end of rnd—42 sts.

Rnd 6: *2 sc into next st, sc into next 6 sts; rep from * to end of rnd—48 sts.

Rnd 7: *2 sc into next st, sc into next 7 sts; rep from * to end of rnd—54 sts.

Rnd 8: *2 sc into next st, sc into next 8 sts; rep from * to end of rnd—60 sts.

- Fasten off and leave a long tail for sewing. Set aside.

MATERIALS AND TOOLS

Red lightweight yarn (refer to page 159 for a list of recommended yarns) (3)

Crochet hook: 2.75 mm (size C-2 U.S.)

Stitch marker

Yarn needle

Polyester fiberfill stuffing

STITCHES AND TECHNIQUES USED

Chain (ch), page 6

Single crochet (sc), page 7

Adjustable ring, page 8

Invisible decrease (invdec), page 12

Top Bed Panel:

Rnds 1–8: Repeat Rnds 1–8 for bottom bed panel.

Rnds 9–11: Sc into each st—60 sts.

- Fasten off and leave a long tail. Sew top bed panel to bottom bed panel. Stuff as you sew up last few stitches. With yarn needle, stitch through both layers to create tufting. Knot yarn and weave in ends.

Bolster:

Rnd 1: Make an adjustable ring, ch 1, work 6 sc into ring. Pull closed—6 sts.

Rnd 2: 2 sc into each st—12 sts.

Rnd 3: *2 sc into next st, sc into 5 sts; rep from * to end of rnd—14 sts.

Rnds 4–63: Sc into each st around.

Rnd 64: *Invdec, sc into next 5 sts; rep from * to end of rnd—12 sts.

- Insert a stitch marker to hold your place. Stuff bolster.

Rnd 65: Invdec around—6 sts.

- Fasten off and leave a very long tail for sewing. Pin bolster around the sides and back of the bed. Sew into place. Weave in ends.

Bowls

Your pet needs her own bowl. For food or water, your pet's own bowl with his or her name makes a cute addition to a personalized gift. Below you'll find patterns for two sizes. A pet dragon will need the large, but your pet hamster will be OK with the smaller one. For tiny pet food, use brown 5-mm pompoms!

Small Bowl:

Rnd 1: Make an adjustable ring, ch 1, 6 sc into ring. Pull tail to close hole—6 sts.

Rnd 2: 2 sc into each st—12 sts.

Rnd 3: *2 sc into next st, sc into next st; rep from * to end of rnd—18 sts.

Rnd 4: *2 sc into next st, sc into next 2 sts; rep from * to end of rnd—24 sts.

Rnd 5: Working into FLO, sc into each st—24 sts.

Rnd 6: Working into both loops of each st, 2 sc into first st, sc into each st around—25 sts.

Rnd 7: 2 sc into first st, sc into next 12 sts, 2 sc into next st, sc into 11 sts—27 sts.

Rnd 8: Working into BLO, sc into each st—27 sts.

Rnd 9: Working into both loops of each st, sc into each st—27 sts.

Rnd 10: Sc into next 12 sts, 2 sc in next st, sc in 14 sts—28 sts.

Rnd 11: *2 sc in next st, sc in next 13 sts; rep from * to end of rnd—30 sts.

Rnd 12: Sc in each st.

- Fasten off and weave in end. Fold into a bowl shape, with the interior of the bowl turning upward at Rnd 5 and back down to form the outer rim of the bowl at Rnd 8.

Large Bowl:

Rnds 1–4: Repeat Rnds 1–4 from small bowl.

Rnd 5: *2 sc into next st, sc in next 3 sts; rep from * to end of rnd—30 sts.

Rnd 6: *2 sc into next st, sc in next 4 sts; rep from * to end of rnd—36 sts.

Rnd 7: Working into FLO, sc into each st—36 sts.

Skill Level:
INTERMEDIATE

MATERIALS AND TOOLS

Lightweight yarn (refer to page 159 for a list of recommended yarns) (3)

Crochet hook: 2.75 mm (size C-2 U.S.)

Stitch marker

Yarn needle

Embroidery floss

Embroidery needle

STITCHES AND TECHNIQUES USED

Adjustable ring, page 8

Chain (ch), page 6

Single crochet (sc), page 7

Front Loops Only (FLO), page 13

Back Loops Only (BLO), page 13

Rnd 8: Working into both loops of each st, sc into each st—36 sts.

Rnd 9: *2 sc into next st, sc in next 17 sts; rep from * to end of rnd—38 sts.

Rnd 10: 2 sc into next st, sc in each st—39 sts.

Rnd 11: 2 sc into next st, sc in each st—40 sts.

Rnd 12: Working into BLO, sc into each st—40 sts.

Rnd 13: Working into both loops of each st, sc into each st—40 sts.

Rnd 14: *2 sc into next st, sc into next 19 sts; rep from * to end of rnd—42 sts.

Rnd 15: Sc into each st.

Rnd 16: *2 sc into next st, sc into next 20 sts; rep from * to end of rnd—44 sts.

Rnd 17: Sc into each st.

- Fasten off and weave in end. Fold into a bowl shape, with the interior of the bowl turning upward at Rnd 7 and back down to form the outer rim of the bowl at Rnd 12.

Finishing:

- With embroidery floss and an embroidery needle, stitch a name on the bowl.

- For a fun touch, add pet food by using the tiniest brown pompoms you can find in the craft store!

Ball

My dog Bear never tires of chasing a ball. Dogs and many other pets just find something irresistible in a bouncing moving object to chase. Crochet this one in a solid color, or use a bright yellow with white stitching for a tennis ball, Bear's favorite.

Skill Level:
INTERMEDIATE

INSTRUCTIONS

Rnd 1: Make an adjustable ring, ch 1, work 6 sc into ring. Pull closed—6 sts. Insert a stitch marker into the loop on your hook. Each time you come back around to the stitch marker, move it up to the loop on your hook to begin the next round.

Rnd 2: 2 sc into each st around—12 sts.

Rnds 3–5: Sc into each st.

- Stuff ball and continue inserting stuffing as you crochet the last round.

Rnd 6: Invdec around—6 sts.

- Fasten off and leave a long tail.

Lightweight yarn (refer to page 159 for a list of recommended yarns) ③

Crochet hook: 2.75 mm (size C-2 U.S.)

Stitch marker

Yarn needle

Embroidery needle (optional, for tennis ball)

White embroidery floss (optional, for tennis ball)

Polyester fiberfill stuffing

STITCHES AND TECHNIQUES USED

Adjustable ring, page 8

Chain (ch), page 6

Single crochet (sc), page 7

Invisible decrease (invdec), page 12

OPTIONAL:

- For a tennis ball, crochet the ball in neon yellow or green. Stitch a continuous curving white line around the ball with white embroidery floss.

Collar

Pets look so fancy when they get a new collar, don't they? I like to buy my dogs different collars for different holidays, and I'm sure I'm not alone in this. Using ribbon makes the collar look like a real one, and also makes it possible to use patterned or themed ribbon for a unique look. Follow the instructions for a tiny tag, and stitch on your pet's initial or just a simple shape, like a heart or star.

Skill Level:
INTERMEDIATE

- Cut a length of ribbon that will fit loosely around your AmiguruME Pet's neck.

- Fold one end of the ribbon over, and stitch one half of the snap fastener into place with matching thread and a thin embroidery needle. Fold the other end of the ribbon back the other way, and stitch the other half of the snap fastener into place. Test that the snaps align and the collar fits around the animal's neck. Slip a jump ring onto the collar for the leash, and place onto your pet's neck.

MATERIALS AND TOOLS

¼-inch satin ribbon

Embroidery needle

Matching thread

¼-inch snap fasteners

10-mm jump ring

OPTIONAL TAG:

- If desired, cut a small circle from felt for a name tag. Poke a tiny hole into the circle; insert another jump ring into the hole; and attach to a second jump ring placed on the collar.

Use a permanent marker or embroidery thread to stitch your pet's initial onto the tag.

• Leash

This crocheted leash will allow you to safely walk your AmiguruME pet. It attaches to the aforementioned collar, so make sure you make one of those first. Easy to find jewelry findings provide the hardware necessary for making this tiny accessory.

INSTRUCTIONS

Row 1: Ch 45. Sl st into 10th ch from hook to form a loop handle. Fasten off.

- Sew lobster clasp to beginning of ch with the starting yarn tail and an

Lightweight yarn (refer to page 159 for a list of recommended yarns) **[3]**

Crochet hook: 2.75 mm (size C-2 U.S.)

Yarn needle

Embroidery needle

10-mm lobster clasp

STITCHES AND TECHNIQUES USED

Chain (ch), page 6

Slip Stitch (sl st), page 7

embroidery needle. Weave in ends.

- To attach leash to collar, place a jump ring on ollar. Clip lobster clasp to jump ring, and take your pet for a walk!

Skill Level:
INTERMEDIATE

Fish Bowl

With easy to find supplies from a craft store, or even a baby food jar, your fish will have a nice place to swim. The size and shape of the bowl is up to you and based on how big your fish turns out to be.

Skill Level:
INTERMEDIATE

INSTRUCTIONS

- Insert tip of pipe cleaner into the bottom of your fish. Bend the pipe cleaner into a stand by folding bottom out and into a ring. Snip off excess.

- Apply super glue sparingly to underside of ring, and insert into the bottom of the jar. Hold into place until dry.

MATERIALS AND TOOLS

Small glass or plastic jar, 2.5 inches (6.4 cm) tall

Pipe cleaner

Super glue

RESOURCES

SMOOTH YARNS

DMC Natura Cotton; sport-weight yarn (2)

Lion Brand Vanna's Choice; worsted-weight yarn (4)

Red Heart Anne Geddes Baby; DK weight yarn (3)

I Love This Yarn Sport; sport-weight yarn (2)

FUZZY YARNS

Yarn Bee Brushworks; DK weight yarn (3)

Lion Brand Vanna's Choice (brushed); worsted-weight yarn (4)

I Love This Yarn Sport (brushed); DK weight yarn (3)

CURLY YARNS

Baby Bee Baby Boucle; DK weight yarn (3)

HOOKS

Clover Amour Hooks

Clover Soft-Touch Hooks

POLYESTER FIBERFILL

Fairfield 100% Polyester Poly-fil

WHERE TO BUY

DMC
dmc.com
1-800-275-4117

Lion Brand Yarn Company
lionbrand.com
1-800-258-YARN

Red Heart Yarns
redheart.com
1-800-648-1479

Hobby Lobby
shop.hobbylobby.com
1-800-888-0321

Jo-ann Fabric and Craft Stores
joann.com
1-888-739-4120

Glass Eyes Online
glasseyesonline.com

6060 Eyes
6060.etsy.com

ACKNOWLEDGMENTS

'd like to thank my family, first and foremost, for the sacrifices you have made all along this fun journey to write this book. Putting the kids to bed, stopping to grab dinner on your way home, and prompting me to stop procrastinating, all the things you've done to help this happen, Paul, my BFF, have made this possible. My boys, Luke, Jack, and Levi, who love looking at the little animals I make and are always ready with a helpful tip or a brutally honest opinion, I thank you guys.

My mom, the Crafty Queen, you've always been supportive and proud, and I love you. Pat and Becky, for the helpfulness and support, thank you! Sisters, thank you for always telling me how cute my stuff is and for being my best friends.

Thank you Kate McKean, the best literary editor, who has guided me through writing two books and continues to amaze me with her ability to multitask.

My editor, Connie Santisteban, for being as excited as I was about starting this book, I thank you. I appreciate your thoughtful opinions and motivation throughout this project. Thank you to my tech editor Rita Greenfeder for your amazingly fast work and helpful insight. Thanks also to the rest of the book team at Sterling. The editing, photos, and layout and design of my book amazes me and I thank you for all of your hard work. It's beautiful.

Thank you to all the supporters I have online! Facebook, Twitter, and Instagram have introduced me to so many of you out there, and I love being able to communicate about our mutual love of all things cute and crafty. All of your shares and likes keep me creating and crocheting.

I feel obligated to thank Netflix, without which I would have spent many hours crocheting while staring at the wall or watching mindless daytime TV instead of happily bingeing on crime documentaries and Kimmy Schmidt.

Last of all, thank you to my furry children, Bear and Kona. You can't read, but I will read this to you one day. You inspired me to give all the other pet parents a way to immortalize their smallest family members. You humor me, you lick me, yes, sometimes you annoy me, and you love me. Please don't chew up this book.

ABOUT THE AUTHOR

Allison Hoffman never met a craft she didn't like. Something about crocheting got her hooked, and she has been making amigurumi for almost 10 years. Her work has been featured on *The Today Show, Conan, Yo Gabba Gabba, Glee,* and *The Martha Stewart Show,* among others, as well as in several magazines, newspaper articles, and online features all over the world. She is the author of *AmiguruME*, published by Sterling Publishing. She exhibits her work in galleries across the United States and has a passion for kitsch and pop culture, which inspires most of her work. She blogs at craftyiscool.com. She and her husband and their three sons live in Austin, Texas, with her real life AmiguruME Pets, two Labs named Kona and Bear.

INDEX